Horses Hate Surprise Parties

Equitation Science for Young Riders

Portland Jones and Sophie Warren

First published in Australia by Portland Jones and Sophie Warren

Herne Hill,
Western Australia
Email: info@swequestrian.com.au
Website: www.sustainableequitation.com.au

Copyright © 2016 - Portland Jones and Sophie Warren

All rights reserved. No part of this publication may be reproduced, stored in a retrieval system, or transmitted in any form by any means, electrons, mechanical, photocopying, recording or otherwise, without the permission of the copyright holders.

ISBN 978-0-646-96232-0

A CIP catalogue record for this book is available from the National Library of Australia.

Published by Portland Jones and Sophie Warren
Design by Portland Jones and Sophie Warren
Illustrations by Barbara Hinchliffe
Training and competition photographs by Mandy Smith and Redfoto
Dedication photo by Melissa Bücheler Photography
Printed by Wide Printing

DISCLAIMER
This book contains material prepared by Portland Jones and Sophie Warren. Please ensure that it is appropriate to your own experience and circumstance before relying on any part of its contents. We will not be liable for any harm to horse, rider or property (including direct and consequential loss and damage) relating to use of this material or reliance upon it.

This book is dedicated to all of the horses that we have known but especially to the mighty Rex.

We have given him our hearts, but the horse, he gives us everything.

FOREWORD

Equitation Science emerged as an academic discipline at the beginning of the 21st century. Drawing on a range of scientific disciplines, it aims to objectively examine the interactions of horses and humans as a way of improving equine welfare and achieving greater efficiency in horse training. Equitation Science uses an evidence-based approach to understanding the ways in which horses and humans interact and has, since its inception, illuminated much that can be improved in modern horse management and training.

One of the most important contributions that Equitation Science has made to equestrian endeavour is to demonstrate the close link between evidence-based training, improved rider safety and horse welfare. That is, research has shown that when used correctly, the scientific principles of learning will help keep riders safe and optimise the welfare of the horse.

Horses Hate Surprise Parties is the first Equitation Science book for young riders. There are many books for young riders about rider position, saddlery and grooming – but this is the first book that will teach them the scientific principles of training their horse. Riders of all ages will appreciate the insights this book offers into horse behaviour and how to correctly use learning theory. The exercises are progressive, easy to follow and clearly explained.

However, the most significant contribution of this book is to make the scientific principles of learning readily available for young riders and this, as research has shown, can help to keep them safe. As such this is not only an enjoyable book, it is also an important one. It is my hope that this book becomes a core text for pony clubs across the world and all other junior equestrian institutions that hold human safety and horse welfare as their highest ideals. I am very pleased to recommend this groundbreaking book. It will most certainly save lives.

Dr Andrew McLean

PhD (Equine Cognition & Learning),
BSc (Zoology), Dip Ed.
CEO - *Equitation Science International*,
Senior Vice Chairman - *Human Elephant Learning Programs.*

What's inside...

Introduction 1

Chapter One - Evolution, domestication and a bunch of old stuff 5

Chapter Two - History and some other really old stuff 11

Chapter Three - How your horse works 17

Chapter Four - The flight response 29

Chapter Five - The horse trainer's tool kit... 37

    Operant Conditioning 39

        Positive Reinforcement 40

        Negative Reinforcement 41

        Positive Punishment 43

        Negative Punishment........................ 44

    Habituation 46

    Shaping 48

    Classical Conditioning 49

    Ten Principles of Training 52

    What are horse surprise parties? 55

Chapter Six - Foundation responses in hand: stop 59

Chapter Seven - Foundation responses in hand: go forward and park 77

Chapter Eight - Foundation responses under saddle: stop 87

Chapter Nine - Foundation responses under saddle: go forwards 103

Chapter Ten - Foundation responses under saddle: turn.............................113

    Direct Turn................................ 116

    Indirect Turn 124

Chapter Eleven - Jumping and other really fun stuff 129

    Poles 132

    Types of show jumps 138

    Jumping at the trot 139

    Jumping at the canter 144

    Exercises to try............................ 145

    Trouble shooting............................ 148

Chapter Twelve - More fun stuff: Cross Country 153

    Types of Cross-Country Jumps............. 155

    Cross-Country Basics......................... 157

Chapter Thirteen - Show-nopoly 163

Introduction

When Neil Armstrong walked on the moon he said, "That's one small step for a man; one giant leap for mankind." Do you think the first person to ride a horse said something clever like Neil, or did they just hold on really tight and yell out some of those words you shouldn't say in front of Grandma? I don't suppose we'll ever know but, either way, that first ride was one of the most important events in human history. Once humans discovered that they could ride horses, our world and the world of the horse, would never be the same again.

> *Once humans discovered that they could ride horses, our world and the world of the horse, would never be the same again.*

A smart person once said that history was written from the back of the horse. It's easy to see why they said it, because humans and horses have been living together for a very long time. Much longer than your life time!

> *A smart person once said that history was written from the back of the horse.*

Horses and humans have lived together for over 6000 years

Horses and humans have lived together for over 6000 years, so it's not at all surprising that we love them. We love the horse so much that sometimes we like to think that he is just like us. A little bit like a slightly silly person inside a furry horse suit. The word for this is anthropomorphism.

Nerd Word Alert!
Anthropomorphism is when human emotions and attitudes are used to describe animals and explain their behaviour. The problem with anthropomorphism is that it's like playing a game of Chinese whispers that has lasted for six thousand years.

There's so much information and so many ideas about horses that it's hard to know what is right, what is wishful thinking, and what is just plain crazy!

There's so much information and so many ideas about horses that it's hard to know what is right, what is wishful thinking and what is just plain crazy. Which is probably why we don't always get horse training right, even though we've been doing it for a long, long time.

But, luckily, science can help us. Equitation Science is a new field of study that uses scientific evidence to determine the best way to train and manage horses. It can tell us where in the past we've got horse training wrong and where we've got it right. It can help us to make good decisions and it can make life much better for the horse.

Equitation science can help us to make good decisions and it can make life much better for the horse.

Equitation Science is like the skinny guy in glasses that goes into a phone booth and flies out wearing a red cape and his underpants on the outside. It can make the world a much better place for horses!

In this book we'll look at how you can use Equitation Science to understand horses and you'll learn how to train and manage them in ways that are good for the horse and good for you. You'll learn why horses hate surprise parties and, most importantly, you'll learn how to avoid them.

4

Chapter One

Evolution, domestication and a bunch of old stuff

The first horses appeared about 55 million years ago. Although they were called eohippus, which means "dawn horse," they could have been called "ugly horse" just as easily. They were about the size of a fox, with a short neck, hump back and squinty eyes. They had three toes on their back feet and four on the front.

They lived in the forest and ate fruit without peeling it, because it's difficult (and rude) to peel fruit with your toes – even if you do have fourteen of them.

Even though horses were around thousands of years ago, they never existed at the same time as dinosaurs.

Even though horses were around thousands of years ago, they never existed at the same time as dinosaurs. The last dinosaurs died out about 70 million years ago, which is quite a while before our ancestors and the first horses appeared. That's pretty lucky because most horses are terrified of a plastic bag blowing in the wind, so imagine how scary a Tyrannosaurus Rex would have been!

Early horses used their large eyes and long, skinny legs to avoid being lunch for other animals.

Over the next few million years horses made themselves at home all over Asia, North America and Europe. They were very successful, evolving to suit a number of different environments including jungle, grassland and forest. All of the horses alive today share a common ancestor that lived about 4 million years ago. These early horses used their large eyes and long, skinny legs to avoid being lunch for other animals and they were very successful until about 25,000 years ago when the Ice Age cooled the whole planet right down.

It's quite likely that if ancient horses hadn't made friends with humans they would have become extinct.

With its massive glaciers and freezing snowstorms, the Ice Age was pretty terrible – unless, of course, you were a woolly mammoth or a mastodon. These big, fat elephant look-alikes had warm, woolly coats and a thick layer of blubber to keep them warm. Not so the poor horse! The Ice Age killed off all the horses in Asia and North America and almost all of the horses in Europe. Archaeologists and people who know about old stuff believe that the horse would have died out completely if it were not for one thing – domestication. It's quite likely that if ancient horses hadn't made friends with humans they would have become extinct.

> ### Nerd Word Alert!
> Archeologists are scientists that look at old things to discover information about the history of humans and animals. They often dig up very old fossils of animal remains to find out what they were like in years gone by.

Even though horses were around thousands of years ago, they never existed at the same time as dinosaurs.

Early horses learned to live near human settlements because the humans chased away really scary predators like wolves and they left food scraps lying around that the horse could scavenge. In return the people often hunted the horse for its meat and hide. But the benefits of living close to people must have been greater than the costs because very soon horses and people were getting along pretty well.

The earliest evidence of domestication comes from fossils that were discovered in what is now modern day Kazakhstan. Archaeologists found the skull of a horse's head and when they looked at it under a microscope they discovered a groove on the front edge of its premolars, which are the teeth just in front of the horse's big chewing ones. This kind of wear is only seen in horses that have had a bit in their mouth because they will often hold the bit between their teeth.

Our ancestors invented bits before they invented the wheel. Amazing!

They also found some carved bits of bone that later turned out to be the sides of a bit. Which means that our ancestors invented bits before they invented the wheel. That's pretty amazing!

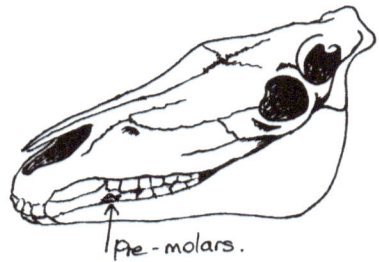

Here's a place for you to write stuff!

Chapter Two

History and some other really old stuff

The first book on horse training was written over 3000 years ago by a fellow called Kikkuli. The book was written before paper was invented and was chiseled onto stone tablets – a bit like an iPad, only much slower and heavier. Kikkuli's chariot horses lived well, even by today's standards. They were stabled, rugged, bathed in warm water, given massages and fed three times a day.

Xenephon was really cool because although he was a soldier he thought that horse training was a form of art and believed in gentle training methods.

The next, and most famous, ancient book about horse training was written almost 1000 years later and is called On Horsemanship. The author, Xenophon, was born in 430BC and was a soldier who went to war on a horse. Amongst many other useful tips in his book Xenophon suggests choosing a horse with a fleshy back. This might seem kind of odd unless you know that Greek soldiers in Xenophon's day rode bareback in short skirts and they hadn't yet invented underpants. So a horse with a bony back and high wither would have been pretty uncomfortable! Xenophon was really cool because although he was a soldier he thought that horse training was a form of art and he believed in gentle training methods.

After Xenophon's era there was a long period of time when horse training was viewed as less of an art and more of a practical skill and it would be many centuries before people once again started to celebrate horse training as something beautiful and not just a good way to go to war.

The next big development in horse training was the invention of the saddle by the Sarmatians in the third century AD. The Sarmatians were fierce nomads who were always fighting other tribes. Not just the men either – Sarmatian women were skilled hunters and brave warriors. Some archaeologists say that the Sarmatian women had to kill two people in battle before they could get married. And their horses were just as tough. Although only about 14hh they could be ridden for many days with very little food and water.

The Sarmatians' horses were tough. They were about 14 hands high and could be ridden for many days with very little food and water.

Over the next few centuries ancient people found many uses for horses and they spread across the developed world. Thanks to the saddle, the cavalry became more and more important. The kind of

13

horse that was bred for war changed as the needs of the cavalry did. In the 1400s medieval knights rode into battle with very heavy, metal armour weighing up to 40kgs. Their horses also wore armour and had to be big and strong to carry all the extra weight. As weapons got lighter, the use of armour was gradually phased out and cavalry horses were bred to be lighter and faster.

The Spanish Riding School gives us an idea of what training might have looked like hundreds of years ago.

In the 1500s horse training came to be seen as a form of entertainment, like music or theatre. In Europe horse training shows were as popular as going to the movies is today. The Spanish Riding School in Vienna was established in 1572 to entertain people and it gives us an idea today of what horse training might have looked like hundreds of years ago.

It seems that human beings will get competitive about just about anything – even eating boiled eggs or three legged racing. So, it was inevitable that horse riding would eventually become competitive too. Horse riding competitions started to gain popularity in the 1800s and an individual jumping contest was included in the Olympic Games for the first time in 1900. The first Olympic dressage competition occurred in 1912. Riders had to walk, trot and canter as well as show halt-to-canter and gallop-to-halt transitions. They also had to jump five high obstacles and one wide one.

There are almost 60 million horses in the world today and more than 350 different breeds.

Today there are almost 60 million horses in the world. There are more than 350 different breeds and they live on every continent except Antarctica. Which is pretty amazing when you consider that without domestication it is quite likely that the only horses around today would be dusty old fossils in museums.

Here's a place for you to write stuff!

Chapter Three

How your horse works

Good science is like a pair of goggles that only sees the truth and it can tell us more than we ever dreamed possible about the world. When we look at the horse with our scientific goggles on we can understand lots about what he can and can't do. That is, we can understand exactly how the horse works.

> *Horses are much better at being just horses than they are at being racehorses, show jumpers or any of the other jobs that they do today.*

Horses are horses because of evolution – a process of gradual change that's been going on for 55 million years. The characteristics that they still have today are there because they helped them to breed and survive in the wild.

Because of evolution horses are really good at forming and maintaining herds, grazing a variety of different grasses and staying away from predators. And because of evolution the horse's brain is really, really different to ours. After 55 million years of evolution, the 6000 years of domestication are just a tiny drop in an enormous ocean of time. Which means that horses are much better at being just horses than they are at being racehorses, show jumpers or any of the other jobs that they do today.

> *After 55 million years of evolution, the 6000 years of domestication are just a tiny drop in an enormous ocean of time.*

Nerd Word Alert!
Evolution explains why animals and plants are so good at surviving in their environments. It is the process of gradual change that makes each animal uniquely suited to its job and way of living. Evolution is a very slow process and adaptations happen over many, many generations.

Horses have amazing memories. But the way that they work is not at all like ours. Horses can't recollect like we can, so they won't travel home from a show wondering if they could have taken jump five a little better. However, if you take them back to the same show ground years later they will remember that the bottom corner of the dressage arena was very near a terribly scary rubbish bin. This is because horse memory is all about survival. For an animal whose life depends on speed, instant reactions are very important. Horses make mental maps of the places they have been to and so unfamiliar things in familiar places make them very suspicious and ready to run away. Try parking something that's familiar to your horse and not very scary (like your wheelbarrow) somewhere it doesn't belong (like the middle of the arena) and watch how he reacts. Most horses' reactions will range from somewhere between intensely curious to completely and utterly terrified.

Horses make mental maps of the places they have been to and so unfamiliar things in familiar places make them very suspicious and ready to run away.

Horses also don't have what psychologists call object permanence. Have you ever played the "boo" game with a baby? From about six months of age human babies love it if you cover your face with your hands and then take them away quickly, because they are learning that just because they can't see something doesn't mean it isn't there. You can't play the "boo" game with a horse because they never develop object permanence – for a horse the saying "out of sight, out of mind" really is true. We'll talk a lot more about the importance of this in the chapter on jumping.

For a horse the saying "out of sight, out of mind" really is true.

Horses are very good at forming habits and there are a few evolutionary reasons why. Habits allow for quick reactions and a fast escape from danger. If a wild horse is frightened, he won't try and work out why, he will just run away because that's what he does. Habits also stay pretty much the same over time and are quick to learn. This means that a young wild horse soon learns how to avoid danger and survive. But the most important reason that horses are good at forming habits is because habits are easier than complicated thinking. Horses are good at lots

Horses are not great at reasoning because grass, unlike mice, cannot hide.

of things but complex thought and logic aren't at the top of the list. A clever scientist once pointed out that the horse is not great at reasoning because grass, unlike mice, cannot hide. And an animal's brain is largely shaped by the challenges it faces to feed itself. Animals tend not to have characteristics that they don't need because evolution is great at getting rid of excess baggage.

Did you know that no-one has ever been able to prove that horses can learn to do new things by watching other horses? Horses will follow each other and often do the same things together (like rolling), but they won't learn new things like piaffe or barrel racing because they have been watching other horses. It used to be believed that crib-biting, windsucking and weaving could be learned - but they're not. These behaviours are called stereotypies and they are a way that horses cope with living in an environment that they aren't evolved for. Nothing in the horse's evolution prepared him for stables, competitions and living without a herd – but these are a fact of life for many modern horses and stereotypies are one of the ways that they cope.

Nothing in the horse's evolution prepared him for stables, competitions and living without a herd.

Horses also don't recognise themselves in a mirror. The scientific test for self-awareness is called a mirror test. Animals that are taking the test are shown a mirror. After a while, the mirror is removed, the

Horses can't learn to do new things by watching other horses do them.

animal is marked with a spot of coloured dye and then the mirror is returned. Chimps, gorillas, orangutans, dolphins and killer whales all show great surprise and curiosity when they look in the mirror and see the dye on themselves. Horses, cats and human babies under 18 months of age fail the mirror test because they show no surprise. Scientists believe that understanding that the mirror is a reflection and not just another animal with dye on its face indicates self-awareness.

Horses have very big eyes on the side of their heads which makes them very hard to sneak up on.

Horses have really good vision and it's quite different to ours. They have very big eyes on the sides of their heads which makes them very hard to sneak up on. They can see far away things better than people can but they don't see colours nearly as well as we do. Horses and dogs are called dichromates because they have two different kinds of colour receptors. Although they can see colours they don't see as many as we do. Horse colour vision is a little bit like looking at the world through a greeny-grey filter. Humans and cats have three different kinds of colour receptor. Cats don't see the same depth of colour as we do, their world is more gently pastel coloured. Birds have four kinds of colour receptor and they can see all of the colours that we can, as well as ultra violet.

Horses have two kinds of vision. When they are relaxed they use their monocular vision and each eye looks around separately. Using monocular vision they can see in an almost full circle with blind spots just in front and just behind them. This is why people say you should never walk up to a horse from directly behind because he might not be able to see you and could get frightened. When horses want to focus on something they use their binocular vision and both eyes look at the same thing. Horses see down the length of their noses so they will often lift their heads when using binocular vision. This is why it's important for horses to be able to lift their heads when jumping – they may not be able to see the fence if their head is lowered or at an unnatural angle.

Horses see down the length of their noses so they will often lift their heads when using binocular vision to focus on objects.

When horses focus on something in the distance they may move their heads up and down or tilt their heads. This is because their pupils are narrow and long, unlike ours which are round. If you want to know what it feels like to be a horse using his binocular vision you can take a pair of glasses (borrow Mum's, she won't mind!) and put dark coloured tape across the top and bottom of the lenses so that just a thin strip (about 15mm wide) is left for you to see through. You'll be surprised at how much you need to move your head to see.

Your horse sees from his nose forwards so he can't see his own chin or what he's eating.

Your horse sees from his nose forwards so he can't see his own chin or what he's eating. That's why he has so many whiskers. These whiskers are called vibrissae and they are extremely sensitive. They have their own blood and nerve supplies and there is a whole section of the horse's brain just for interpreting the information that they gather. They help to keep the horse safe because they help him judge distances, particularly at night or in tight spaces like a trailer. Horses can't see the bits of grass that they're grazing so their vibrissae help them to choose between weeds and pasture.

Your horse's large, mobile ears work like small, furry satellite dishes that can tell not only what is making the sound, but also where it is coming from and from how far away.

Did You Know?
In some countries it is illegal to cut or trim your horse's whiskers. It's just as well because they are very important to the horse and should always be left natural.

As well as great vision the horse also has extremely sensitive hearing. His large, mobile ears can rotate independently, a little bit like small, furry satellite dishes. He can not only tell what is making the sound, he can also tell where it is coming from and from how far away. Noisy environments like shows and roadsides can be very stressful for horses because their hearing is so good.

If it sounds loud to you it is probably almost unbearably loud for your horse. Police horses that work in very noisy places sometimes wear ear-plugs to lessen the stress caused by loud noises.

Although his sense of hearing is far better than ours it is the horse's sense of smell that is quite extraordinary. It is hard to say exactly but some scientists have estimated that the horse can smell 1000 times better than we can. The horse uses his flexible, moist nostrils to catch scent molecules. If something smells particularly interesting he will curl his top lip upward and raise his head. This is called flehmen and although he looks like he's laughing, he's actually just keeping the scent molecules inside his nose for longer. Horses can't vomit so their amazing sense of smell helps them to avoid eating spoiled or poisonous food. It also helps them to detect the approach of hungry predators and even to sense when you are on your way with the feed bucket!

Scientists have estimated that the horse can smell 1000 times better than we can!

Lots of people talk to their horses and some of them think that the horse understands what they are saying. And while it is true that horses will learn to do things like "whoa" and "back up" when told to do so they aren't actually learning to speak the same language as us, they are performing behaviours from word cues. It's quite a big difference – language is a complicated system for two-way communication and word cues are the result of training. You could just as easily train your horse to go backwards using

Horses can perform behaviours from word cues but this doesn't mean they are learning to speak our language.

the command "fly" or to slow from the command "giddy up". This is because he doesn't understand the meaning of the word, it just becomes associated with a behaviour.

We make and store language in the big front section of our brains known as the pre-frontal cortex, and horses don't have this part. Expecting them to understand human language is a little bit like going to the corner store expecting to be able to buy a nuclear reactor. Complex human emotions also develop in the pre-frontal cortex, as do personality traits like laziness or greed. The horse, because he doesn't have this part of the brain, can't show these things and he doesn't worry about things like the future, religion or fashion, either. His brain is not a lesser version of ours, it is uniquely his and perfectly adapted for the job of finding food, bonding with other horses and staying safe.

The horse doesn't worry about things like the future, religion or fashion.

Their brains are uniquely theirs and perfectly adapted for the job of finding food, bonding with other horses and staying safe.

Did You Know?
Your horse can sleep standing up. He has a unique system in his hind legs that allows them to more or less lock in the upright position. He can sleep standing up like this for up to five hours a night and will usually lie down for another couple of hours of deeper sleep.

Nerd Word Alert!

The pre-frontal cortex is a section of the human brain that stores language and complex human emotions such as love, jealousy and personality traits like laziness and greed. The horse doesn't have this section of his brain which makes his life much more simple in many ways.

If we look at the scientific evidence we can see that the horse's world is not at all like ours. Just as the horse's brain is uniquely adapted for his life as a grazer, our human brains are adapted for life as hunters and gatherers. Our ancestors relied on their large, complex brains for survival, just as the horse's ancestors relied on their acute senses, habits and speed. How can we guess what life is like for an animal that looks in a mirror and doesn't realise that what he sees is himself? The horse's world is so different to our own – yet it is all too easy to assume that we know what he is thinking and feeling.

> *The horse's world is very different to ours....how can we guess what life is like for an animal that looks in a mirror and doesn't realise that what he sees is himself?*

When we train the horse it is easy to get frustrated because we believe that the horse should know what he is being asked to do, isn't trying hard enough or is being naughty. But we don't really know those things, they are just guesses that we make when we are not wearing our scientific goggles.

When we put on our scientific goggles we can see that while there are lots of things that the horse can do better than we can, he can't pretend to be something that he isn't. He can't be greedy or lazy or have complex emotions like jealousy or ambition. He can't solve complex problems and he can't use language like we can. Maybe one day the horse will be able to speak to us and do fractions, but it's best not to be in a hurry because evolution works slowly, so we might have to wait awhile – probably at least a million years or so.

Chapter Four

The flight response

Horses evolved to live in herds made up of mares, their offspring and one or more stallions. People used to believe that the stallion was the boss of the herd and all the other horses were arranged below him, kind of like the ranks in an army. We now know that the way horses get on and work out their differences is a lot more complicated and changeable. In fact, the role of boss horse is shared by lots of different horses depending on the situation. One horse might be the boss at the waterhole and another might be the boss when it comes to new grass.

> *The role of boss horse is usually shared - one horse might be the boss at the waterhole and another when it comes to new grass.*

Some people have tried to use herd structure (sometimes called herd dynamics) when training their horses but it's a bit of a funny idea. Not only because the boss in the horse herd changes depending on the situation but also because horses use their whole bodies to communicate. The signals they use are usually so small and quick that most people can't even see them unless they are filmed and replayed in slow motion. Just the flick of an ear, a twitch of a nostril or the raising of a tail can mean something to another horse. Training based on herd dynamics tends to focus on chasing and obviously (because people have short necks, short

noses, ears that don't move and no tails) misses out on all the other really important stuff. It's a bit like going to a foreign country and trying to communicate using only swear words!

> *Training using herd dynamics is a bit like going to a foreign country and trying to communicate using only swear words.*

The bonds or friendships shared by horses in herds are extremely important. In the wild a horse on its own is very likely to get eaten by a predator, so making and keeping friends is vital. Bonding is so important that horses have a small patch of skin at the base of their necks (just below the wither) that, when scratched and rubbed, will calm them if they are excited. Because the horse can't reach this spot on his own it has to be scratched by another horse and this mutual grooming deepens the attachment between herd members. Try scratching your own horse at the base of his neck – you might have to keep going for a few minutes but eventually he will relax and show signs that he is enjoying it.

> *You can use scratching at the base of the neck as a reward when you are riding or handling your horse.*

You can use scratching at the base of the neck as a reward when you are riding or handling your horse. Horses don't pat or slap each other, for most of them patting is something to put up with, rather than something to be enjoyed. Try scratching your horse instead, he'll enjoy it much more.

The instinct to run away from danger is called the flight response.

One of the things that the horse does best is running away from danger. There are few animals on the planet as fast as a galloping horse and their senses are very sharp so they can see, smell and hear danger approaching. The instinct to run away from danger is called the flight response and it influences a great deal of the horse's behaviour. Anyone who keeps, trains or rides a horse should understand how the flight response works because managing it is the best way to keep yourself safe and your horse happy.

The more the horse expresses the flight response, the more likely he is to do it again.

Scientists call the part of the brain that sorts out what is scary and what isn't the amygdala. Of all the large, domesticated mammals the horse has the biggest amygdala and, in a way, it is this that drives the flight response.

> ### Nerd Word Alert!
> The amygdala is the part of the brain that sorts out scary stuff, from not so scary stuff. It is a pretty important part of the horse's brain because it helps to keep him from being another animal's lunch.

Long term flight response can lead to what scientists call hyper vigilance. This is when a horse is always alert and can't seem to relax.

The more the horse expresses the flight response the more inclined he is to do it again. It's like a snowball – it starts small but it gets much bigger as it goes along. For domestic horses that don't need to run away to survive, the flight response is not a good thing, especially during training. Long term flight response can lead to what scientists call hyper vigilance – this is when the horse is always alert and can't seem to relax. Horses that are expressing the flight response under saddle will try to go faster at every opportunity. They will not maintain a steady rhythm. They are tight through their bodies, they often carry their heads unnaturally high and they might shy, buck or even launch into the air.

When jumping horses are well trained they shouldn't speed up or slow down at their fences.

The flight response is a little bit like a red sock in a load of white washing - even just a little bit can affect the whole horse, and not in a positive way.

It used to be thought that jumping horses that rushed their obstacles just loved to jump, but now we know that speeding up is just one way that the flight response shows up under saddle. A horse that takes off on the cross country course is expressing the flight response just as clearly as one that is running away from a hungry lion. When jumping horses are well trained they shouldn't speed up or slow down at their fences, they should keep the same rhythm in the approach and after the fence.

When it comes to the flight response, prevention is definitely the best cure.

A horse that rushes when jumping is exhibiting the flight response just as clearly as one that is running away from a hungry lion.

No matter what you want to do with your horse, calmness should be your ultimate goal.

The flight response is a little bit like a red sock in a load of white washing – even just a little bit can affect the whole horse, and not in a positive way. Expressions of the flight response can lead to behaviour problems like shying and bucking. They may lead to the development of behaviours like crib-biting and fence walking or to general anxiety and an inability to put on weight. Scientists also believe that stomach ulcers, colic and other tummy upsets can also be worsened by the stress that follows regular expressions of the flight response.

So, what is the best way to prevent the flight response?

The most important thing to understand about the flight response is that it almost always involves the horse's legs moving quickly. Therefore gaining control over your horse's legs is the first step in limiting the flight response and reducing stress. When it comes to the flight response, prevention is definitely the best cure.

If you can control the legs of your horse with light signals he will be obedient and calm.

In the chapters that follow we will show you how the horse learns and how to gain control over your horse's legs. If you can control the legs of your horse he will be obedient. But if you can control the legs of your horse with light signals he will be obedient and calm. No matter what you want to do with your horse, calmness should be your ultimate goal.

Chapter Five

The horse trainer's tool kit

> *Good horse training might look like magic, but it's mostly just consistent practice.*

Have you ever watched one of those programs where they show you how famous magicians do their tricks? It turns out that no matter how incredible the tricks are, they're not magic after all – they're just the result of hard work and practice. Good horse training is just the same, it might look like magic but it's mostly just consistent practice.

All of the behaviours that horses do under saddle are the result of just six responses: stop, go forward, move the shoulders left and right, move the hindquarters left and right. We call these the foundation responses because they form the foundation of the horse's future training. We train the six foundation responses using operant conditioning. Operant conditioning is probably the most important tool in the horse trainer's tool-kit. But there are others including habituation (which is just a fancy word for 'getting used to') and classical conditioning. Once your tool-kit is full and you understand exactly how your horse learns, training will become much easier, for both of you.

> *Operant conditioning is probably the most important tool in the horse trainer's tool kit.*

Nerd Word Alert!
The science of learning is littered with nerdy, big words. They won't impress your horse but they might just impress your friends.

Operant Conditioning

Operant Conditioning is the most important tool for horse trainers to understand as it explains all about reward and punishment. There are two kinds of reward (which are known as reinforcement) and two kinds of punishment. In the table below you can see how it works.

Positive Reinforcement	Positive Punishment
Adding something the horse likes increases a behaviour.	Adding something that the horse doesn't like decreases a behaviour.
Negative Reinforcement	Negative Punishment
Taking away something that the horse doesn't like increases a behaviour.	Taking away something the horse likes decreases a behaviour.

Operant conditioning explains all about reward and punishment.

Positive Reinforcement

Giving your horse something that he likes after a behaviour makes him more likely to do it again. For example, scratching the horse on the neck or giving him a carrot when you've caught him makes him more likely to be caught again.

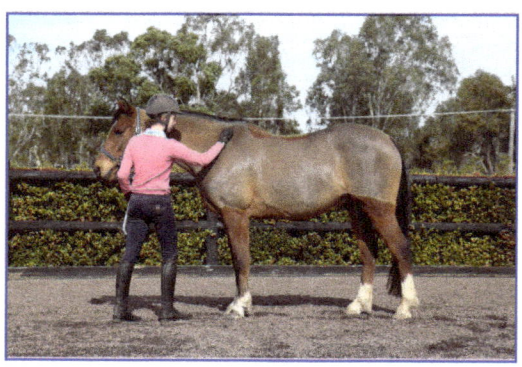

Positive reinforcement is very good for improving behaviours and increasing calmness.

Positive reinforcement is very good for improving behaviours and increasing calmness. In the chapter on ground work we'll talk about using lots of scratches when teaching your horse to park. It's important to remember, however, that the reward must be given at the exact moment the horse does what you want him to do. If you lead your horse back to the stable after you ride him and give him a carrot, you are not reinforcing his good behaviour during the ride, you are reinforcing what he did just before he ate the carrot.

It is important to remember that the reward must be given at the exact moment of the desired behaviour.

Negative Reinforcement

Taking away something the horse doesn't really like after a behaviour makes him more likely to do it again. For example, applying pressure to the reins when the horse is walking and releasing the pressure once he stops makes him more likely to stop again when there is pressure on the reins. The pressure used in negative reinforcement should start off very light, increase gradually and should only be removed when the horse performs the right behaviour.

The pressure in negative reinforcement should start off very light, increase gradually, and should only be removed when the horse performs the right behaviour.

Negative reinforcement is the most important tool in the horse rider's tool-kit. Any form of training that uses pressure, is using negative reinforcement. When you lead or ride your horse you are using negative reinforcement because the cues that you use involve pressure. When horse training goes wrong it is usually because negative reinforcement has been used incorrectly. Because horses are good at forming associations, once trained the pressure used in negative reinforcement can (and should) be very light.

Once trained, the pressure used in negative reinforcement should be very light.

41

We can think of the cues we use in negative reinforcement as having three parts. The first part is a light signal which grows in strength to become a heavier signal (the second part) and the third part is the release. The most important part of the cue is the release. This is because it is the release that tells the horse what he did was correct.

Negative reinforcement cues have three parts: the light signal, the heavier signal and the release of the signal.

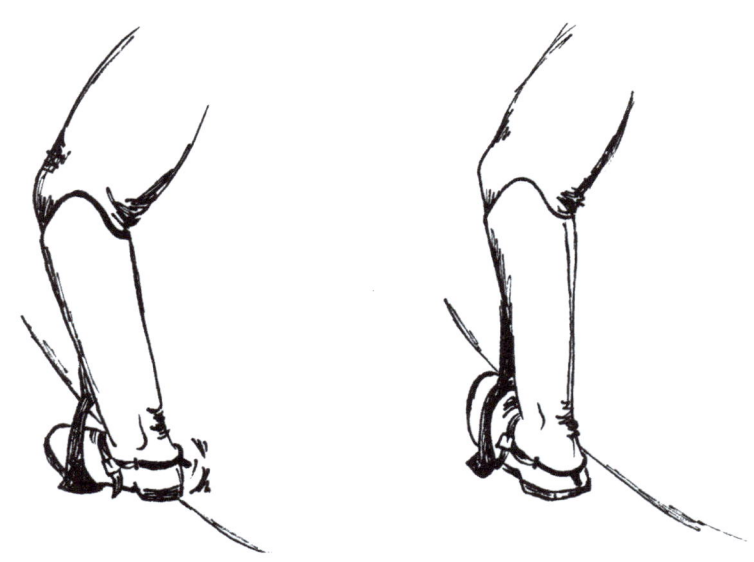

Nerd Word Alert!
As you can see from the operant conditioning table, both forms of reinforcement increase behaviour and both kinds of punishment decrease it. When scientists use the terms positive and negative they use them in the mathematical sense. That is, positive means adding something and negative means taking it away. They don't mean good and bad.

Positive Punishment

Adding something that the horse doesn't like after a behaviour makes him less likely to do it again. For example, getting shocked by an electric fence makes the horse less likely to touch the fence in future.

You should think very carefully before using any kind of punishment in training.

You should think very carefully before you use any kind of punishment in training. It doesn't give the horse any clues as to what to do instead of the incorrect behaviour. For example, if you smack the horse on the nose for biting he might try something that you like even less, like rearing. Also, horses can form powerful associations between punishment and the thing that punished them. As an example, a lot of horses are frightened of the white tape used for electric fences if they have been shocked once or twice, because they have formed an association between the shock and the tape. In the same way, if you use punishment regularly in your training the horse could learn to be frightened of you.

If you use punishment regularly in your training the horse could learn to be frightened of you.

It is far more useful in almost all situations to use negative reinforcement instead of positive punishment. So, if your horse nips when you tighten the girth, it is better to use negative reinforcement to step him back or lower his head than giving him a smack, because it targets the behaviour you want, not just the one you don't want. If you smack the horse for nipping it only teaches him what not to do, it teaches him nothing about the way you want him to behave.

Negative reinforcement is usually more effective than punishment because it targets the behaviour you want, not just the behaviour you don't want.

Negative Punishment

Taking away something that the horse likes after a behaviour makes him less likely to do it again. For example if you are scratching the horse and he tries to bite, if you stop scratching him, he will be less likely to bite next time he's getting a scratch. Negative punishment is not often used by horse trainers but is often used by parents. Have you ever had your mobile phone taken away because you were naughty? Your parents were using negative punishment because they took away something that you like.

A note on reinforcement and timing...

In the last chapter we looked at the horse's brain and talked about how he isn't very good at complex thought. This means that if he refuses to be caught he's not doing it to annoy you – even though it might seem like he is. Because of this you must have very good timing when you train him. Each behaviour has a very, very small window of opportunity for reinforcement or punishment, maybe only one second. If your horse bucks you off, it's no use catching him and punishing him because it's far too late, you're only punishing him for being caught. When using negative reinforcement the pressure must be released at the exact instant the horse does what you want him to do – not five seconds afterwards. The same goes for positive reinforcement. The reward must be given as the horse performs the correct behaviour.

One of the world's best animal trainers, Bob Bailey, says that you get the behaviour you reinforce, not the behaviour you want. The horse will work very hard to get what he wants and one of the things that he wants the most is to remove pressure from his body. So, the most important part of each signal is not when you apply the signal, but when you take it off. If you think about it, training is a lot like photography. Take an imaginary photograph of what your horse did the split second before you took your signal off – that's the behaviour you have reinforced. That's the behaviour you have trained. You need to be really clear about exactly what you want your horse to do and release your pressure cue as soon as he does it.

Each behaviour has a very small window of opportunity for reinforcement or punishment.

You get the behaviour you reinforce, not necessarily the behaviour you want.

Habituation

Now that we've got operant conditioning covered we can move on to some other ways that horses learn. Habituation is just a sciencey way of saying "getting used to". As part of their training, riding horses have to habituate to lots of things like the saddle, the weight of the rider, the wind in the trees and cars on the road. When trained correctly, most horses will habituate pretty quickly to the everyday things in their environment. However, some things are harder to habituate to. Things that are too close (like clippers in the ears), things that move in a crazy way (like kangaroos) or things that appear suddenly (like a plastic bag blowing in the wind) take quite a lot of getting used to.

The quickest way to get your horse to habituate to something

The quickest way to get your horse to habituate to something is to introduce him to it gradually, while still keeping control of his legs.

is to introduce him to it gradually, while still keeping control of his legs. If you want to get your horse used to clippers, it's not a good idea to turn the clippers on and let the horse run away. When this happens the horse just learns to run away from the clippers and every time he practises the flight response he gets better at it.

You can use a technique called counter conditioning to get the horse used to scary things. To do this you turn the clippers on and then immediately give the horse a reward like a carrot. If you repeat this enough times the horse will predict that the sound of clippers means a carrot is coming and he will gradually lose his fear of them.

Most horses will habituate pretty quickly to everyday things in their environment.

Nerd Word Alert!
Habituation is just a sciencey way of saying "getting used to". Horses are quite good at getting used to things, like the saddle and bridle, their rugs, and being near humans.

Another really effective technique for habituation is called overshadowing. Your horse can't multi-task, which means he can only do one thing at a time. During overshadowing the horse is asked to respond to cues that have already been trained (such as stop and go forwards) while something new is introduced. Because he can only focus on one thing at a time he will gradually habituate to the new thing. We'll talk about overshadowing in more detail in the next chapter.

Shaping

Shaping describes the process of gradually changing behaviours so that they get better and better over time. For example, when you first teach a young foal to lead, you wouldn't expect it to walk perfectly beside you on the first attempt. Rather, by rewarding better and better versions of leading you gradually change and improve the behaviour. Apparently Michelangelo, the famous artist, said that he didn't think sculpting was very hard – he simply took a hammer, a chisel and a great big block of marble and chipped off all the excess marble until what he had left was a beautiful statue. That's a really good way to think about training a horse. You just get rid of all the behaviours that you don't want (like shying, bucking and baulking at jumps) until what you're left with is a well trained horse.

Shaping is the process of gradually changing behaviours so that they get better and better over time. You can think of it like making a sculpture.

The most important thing to remember about shaping behaviours is that controlling the legs of your horse with light cues is much more important than controlling where his head goes or trying to work out what he's thinking. We can't possibly imagine what our horse is thinking so we should concentrate on achieving obedience and calmness in every training situation.

Classical Conditioning

Classical conditioning is when an association is formed between a new signal and a response. Here's an example... If you open a bag of carrots and give your horse some, pretty soon he'll hear the crackle of the bag and rush over to get a carrot. An association has been formed between the crackling sound and the carrot. The crackling sound has been classically conditioned to mean that carrots are on their way.

Classical conditioning is when an association is formed between a new signal and a response.

You might have heard of Pavlov's dogs. In the early years of the twentieth century, Russian scientist Ivan Pavlov conducted experiments on dogs to try and learn more about the way that they digest their food. Every day his assistant would bring the dogs some food and Pavlov would measure the amount of saliva that they produced. Apparently Pavlov's assistant had a trolley with a squeaky wheel and, pretty soon, the dogs would start to slobber and drool (salivate) as soon as they heard the trolley squeaking down the hall outside the laboratory.

Pavlov's dogs quickly formed an association with the squeaking sound of the food trolley's wheels and the arrival of their dinner.

Nerd Word Alert!
Ivan Pavlov was a very famous Russian. He was all set for a career as a priest until he read Charles Darwin's book, The Voyage of the Beagle (which, funnily enough, is not about a dog that goes on holiday, but about evolution) and decided to become a scientist.

Pavlov was very interested in this and he decided to do an experiment to work it out. He rang a bell and then fed the dogs. After several repetitions when he rang the bell the dogs would drool as if they were expecting food. Pavlov called what he had discovered classical conditioning.

Seat, weight and voice cues work in horse training because they become associated with other cues that have been trained by operant conditioning.

Seat, weight and voice cues work in horse training because they become associated (because of classical conditioning) with other cues that have been trained by operant conditioning. Here's an example... When you ride, your seat moves in time to the horse's movement, as you slow your horse with the reins your seat moves less. Your horse very quickly learns that less movement from your seat means that the rein signal for slow down is coming and he will slow down when he feels your seat slow. And the opposite is also true – when your horse feels the movement of your seat increase, he will often speed up. The same is true for the word "whoa." The horse is not born understanding that this word means slow down but, over time, he learns to associate "whoa" with slowing signals from the reins and lead rope. So pretty soon the word "whoa" will cause him to slow down.

The horse is not born knowing that the word "whoa" means slow down.

Over his lifetime the horse learns many, many classically conditioned cues. He will start to get excited when he sees the feed room door open, he will neigh when he sees you in the morning and he will be wary of the vet. Classical conditioning is a really important part of training if you understand it and use it well. It is, however, worth remembering that Pavlov's dogs stopped drooling when the bell was rung after a few repetitions without being given any meat. Which means that your seat won't work if the horse is not also obedient to your leg and rein cues. Plus, Pavlov fed the dogs something they really liked, not broccoli. I doubt they would have salivated much at all for broccoli! So, if you want to make sure your seat is an effective cue, make sure your horse stops obediently and lightly from the reins first.

> **Classically conditioned behaviours are like remote controlled toy cars. You have to keep charging them in order for them to work.**

Classically conditioned behaviours are like remote controlled toy cars. You have to keep charging them in order for them to work. With classically conditioned behaviours you have to keep on making the connection between the operant behaviour (like your rein signals) and the classically conditioned cue (like "whoa") otherwise they simply stop working.

Ten Principles of Training

Now that we know how training works we can look at the ten most important rules for horse training. Two very clever scientists, Dr Andrew McLean and Professor Paul McGreevy developed these rules and they are pretty easy to understand and apply. It doesn't matter what kind of riding you do, it's worth sticking to them every day.

1 The horse's brain is very different from ours. His memory, senses and way of learning are very different too. Understand these differences and always remember them when training. For example horses can't pretend or tell lies and they never do things just to annoy you – even if sometimes you might think that they are doing all three.

2 Know how training works. Understand the most important scientific principles, in particular – operant conditioning, habituation, classical conditioning and shaping.

3 Every signal that you use in training should be different and distinct so that there is no confusion for the horse. For example, the signal you use for turn should be easily distinguished from the signal for go and the signal for stop.

4 Don't have unrealistic expectations when you are first training responses. Reward small improvements and understand that the shaping process takes time. Remember what Michelangelo said about sculpting and take very small chips from the block of marble every day.

5 Horses can't multi-task so you should only ever give one cue at a time. For example, don't ask for stop and go at the same time because this is impossible for the horse and causes stress.

6 Each signal should produce only one response. For example, pressure on both reins should only ever cause the horse to slow his legs, it shouldn't also be used to ask the horse to lower his head.

7 Be consistent with your horse at all times, both on the ground and under saddle. Be clear about what it is that you want him to do so that he develops consistent habits. The rules should never change!

8 Make self carriage a priority every day and at every stage of training. This means that you should train your horse to maintain the speed you want while he is being lead and ridden. That is, that he doesn't need to constantly be asked to go forwards or to slow down. Aim to control your horse with light pressure cues.

9 Learn what the flight response looks like. Understand that it is a problem and learn how to control it during training.

10 Having a calm and obedient horse should be your ultimate goal at all times.

What are horse surprise parties and how can you avoid them?

As we've discussed, the horse isn't very good at complex thought. He's happiest when everything stays pretty much the same and he is calmest and most content when his life is predictable. You cannot control the weather or the dog next door but you can help your horse's life to be predictable through clear training.

> *You cannot control the weather or the dog next door but you can help your horse's life to be predictable through clear training.*

Classical conditioning is really important to the horse because it allows him to predict what is coming. He predicts that it is almost dinner time when he sees you with a bucket and a hay net. He predicts that you are going to apply pressure to the reins when your seat slows down. Correctly applied negative reinforcement also allows the horse to predict what is coming because very light pressure precedes (or comes before) heavier pressure. The horse can predict that stronger pressure follows lighter pressure so he learns how to avoid stronger pressure. He learns that stopping from a very light squeeze on the reins means that he avoids stronger rein pressure. He learns that stepping forwards from a very light leg pressure means he avoids a stronger leg pressure.

Classical conditioning is really important because it helps the horse predict what is coming.

Habituation also helps make your horse's life predictable because he gets used to the things that cause him no harm. So, while the clippers may initially cause alarm, over time, when they no longer cause his legs to quicken, he learns to ignore them. Shaping also keeps life predictable because when you understand that training must be gradual and progressive (step by step) there are few sudden changes for the horse. Each day's training builds on the previous day's training. There are very few surprises in a good training system.

There are very few surprises in a good training system.

As we've already discussed, the horse's brain is very different to ours. We have a big prefrontal cortex and we can cope with a little bit of unpredictability. Lots of people love surprise parties because they're exciting and different. Your horse would hate surprise parties for exactly that reason – he has spent pretty much all of his evolution (that's 55 million years), running away from things that are exciting and different. Without a prefrontal cortex for reasoning and complex emotions, surprises are scary. When you use the science of learning correctly you become predictable – and that's a very good thing for your horse.

> **Without a prefrontal cortex for reasoning and complex emotions, surprises are scary.**

In this chapter we've looked at the ways horses learn. If you think about it, almost all forms of learning make the horse's life more predictable. But there's one big exception... can you think what it is? If you said punishment, you're absolutely right. Punishment doesn't allow the horse to change his behaviour to avoid pressure, it just happens. The horse doesn't know the difference between right and wrong, so to him punishment is unpredictable and very unpleasant. You should think very carefully before using punishment when training your horse because it's a surprise party of the very worst kind.

Punishment is a surprise party of the very worst kind.

The really important thing to remember about the horse is that he didn't ask to be trained and, therefore, it is our job as horse owners to make training as enjoyable and stress free as possible.

The horse didn't ask to be trained, so it is very important that we make training as enjoyable and stress free as possible.

Love and other mushy stuff...
People often wonder if their horse loves them and it's a good question. We cannot know what the horse feels or thinks so science can't really answer that question yet. But what we do know is that animals and people form strong bonds to things that give them comfort and care. This is called attachment and it's very important to your horse's wellbeing. Horses that live in herds form strong attachments to their herd mates because they spend a lot of time together and do things like grooming each other. Your horse is most likely to form a strong bond with you if you are always clear and consistent with your training and if you offer comfort in the form of scratching and stroking. Horses love to be touched, especially at the base of the wither and on their necks. Some horses take a while to relax enough to enjoy scratching but if you're patient, you'll soon find that your horse will seek it out. Using touch as a reward for good behaviour is not only good training it will also strengthen the bond between you.

Chapter Six

Foundation responses in hand: stop

> *The ground work training that you do with your horse is like the pre-flight check that pilots do before take-off.*

Before take off, the pilot always checks her plane thoroughly because, if the wings are falling off, it's too late to fix them once the plane is in the air. The ground work training that you do with your horse is quite a lot like the pre-flight check that pilots do before they fly because it allows you to assess your horse's foundation responses and gives you time to fix things before you mount up. But it's even more important than that. Having clear foundation responses is very important to your horse's well-being because it makes his life predictable and saves him from surprise parties. Our aim is to be able to control our horse with light signals and there's no better place to start than with ground work.

> *Foundation responses are like the concrete foundation your house is built on.*

When a horse displays a problem behaviour, equitation scientists can tell us which of his foundation responses are faulty – without even seeing the horse! Behaviours like bucking and rearing almost always start with problems in the foundation responses. That's one of the reasons they're called foundation responses because they're like the concrete foundation that your house sits on. In the next few chapters we'll look at how to correctly train your horse's responses and we'll also look at the problem behaviours that might be associated with failures in each of those responses.

Before you begin ground work training you should have all the right equipment. You should wear a helmet and boots (as well as your other clothes, or you might get a bit cold). Your horse should wear a well fitted head-collar with a lead rope attached or his bridle.

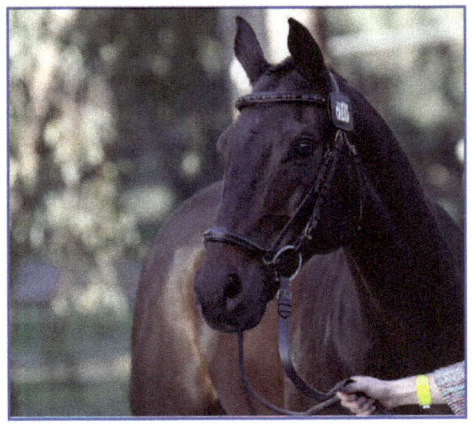

Gloves are optional, though usually a good idea and lots of people like them because you can buy them in pretty colours – though your horse won't notice because his colour vision isn't very good. You'll also need a safe, enclosed area to work in, and you should carry a dressage whip, though if you and your pony are both very small a riding crop will be fine.

You should always wear your helmet and boots when doing ground work.

A note on whips...

Some people don't like to use whips because they think that they are unkind. You aren't going to hurt your horse with your whip, it's just a way of making your arm seem longer. If you can put the palms of your hands on the ground without bending over you probably don't need a whip, but for the rest of us with normal length arms, a whip makes training much easier. It helps to make sure your horse is not frightened of the whip by rubbing it gently all over him while keeping him standing still.

61

You must keep applying the signal until your horse does what you want him to do - otherwise you'll have trained him to do the wrong thing!

You'll be using both negative and positive reinforcement during ground work so we'll brush up on both of them before we begin. To use negative reinforcement, you apply a light pressure that gets stronger and stronger until the horse does what you want him to do then you stop it immediately. It's useful to think of it as happening in three phases: the first phase is the light signal (this is like saying "please"). The second phase is the stronger signal (this is like saying "do it now") and the third phase is the release of pressure (which is like saying "thank you very much"). The third phase of the signal is the most important part because it's the release that tells the horse that what he did was correct. So make sure that you don't stop applying your pressure until your horse does what you want him to do – otherwise you'll have accidentally trained him to do the wrong thing!

In our ground work training we'll be using both rein and whip pressure to apply negative reinforcement. We must never hurt the horse with either of these; at their heaviest, both pressures should only ever be mildly uncomfortable. During training, if you want to increase the rein pressure, you can lightly vibrate the reins because this kind of pressure is hard for the horse to ignore. The whip should never be used to hit the horse but rather should lightly tap him, increasing the speed of the taps, not the pressure. This type of signal is annoying and hard to ignore but isn't painful. Before you begin training you can practise your whip tapping skills on your younger brother or sister…they won't mind at all!

The whip should never be used to hit the horse but rather should lightly tap him, increasing the speed of the taps, not the pressure.

The pressure you use for negative reinforcement should increase gradually – just like turning up the volume on the radio. It should always start lightly and increase in intensity until the horse does what you want him to do. Then it goes away completely. So, when you want your horse to stop you apply light pressure on the reins, increasing the pressure until he stops and then releasing it completely. Holding the cue for stop on all of the time is a little bit like driving a car with the handbrake on – eventually the brakes wear out. It's much better to gradually train your horse to maintain his own speed than to try and keep holding him with constant pressure.

The pressure you use for negative reinforcement should increase gradually - like turning the volume up on the radio.

As well as negative reinforcement, we'll also be using positive reinforcement during training which means we will scratch the horse and stroke him immediately after he offers the right behaviour. It's a great idea to spend some time scratching and stroking your horse before we begin so that you can discover what is reinforcing for him. You'll know you've found the right place when he starts to make funny faces. Look for chewing and lip licking or a long top lip with maybe some slow blinking too because they are all signs that you've found the right spot.

The stop response is really important because it can help prevent the flight response and so keeps us safe.

If your horse is tense when you lead him, jogs, rushes or barges over the top of you it is very likely that he has a problem with his stop response in hand.

Nerd Word Alert!
Foundation responses are like the concrete foundations your house is built on. They are the building blocks for the rest of your training which is why they are so important.

The stop response is really important because it helps prevent the flight response which helps keep us safe. This is why it is the first foundation response that you're going to train. It has three parts – step back, stop and slow. To begin with we'll check step back because it's the easiest to achieve. Our goal with this exercise is to be able to produce two steps backwards from one light signal.

Start by standing in front of your horse's left shoulder, facing him with the reins (or lead rope) in your left hand. Without moving your legs, apply pressure on the reins towards his wither and assess how much pressure you have to apply before he takes a single, backwards step. How heavy is your horse? Is he as heavy as a small chocolate bar? As heavy as a carton of milk? Or as heavy as a lawn mower? If you've got a milk carton, a lawn mower or maybe something even heavier, like an iceberg – we've definitely got work to do! But don't worry, with the correct training all horses can become chocolate bars.

With correct training, all horses can become light in their responses.

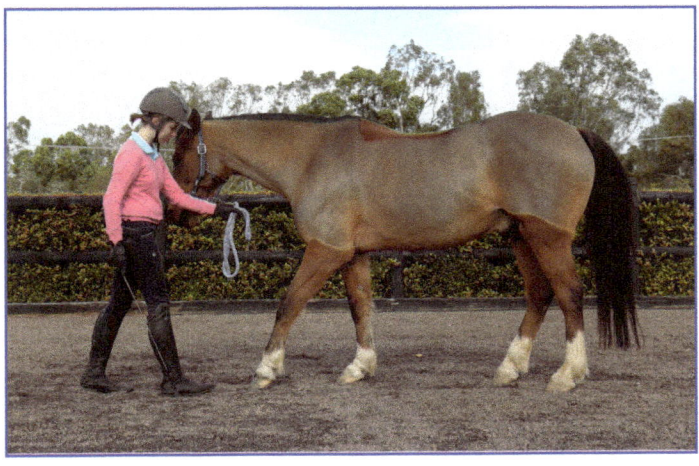

Without moving your legs, apply pressure on the reins towards his wither and assess how much pressure you have to apply before he takes a backwards step.

To train a lighter step back response you can train your horse to step back from a different pressure and then pair that new response with the rein signal using classical conditioning. It sounds complicated but it's not really! Using your whip, tap your horse on the cannon bone of his front leg, just below the knee. Tap the leg that is the most forward (because this is the one that will step backwards first). As soon as he takes one step

Your whip taps should be quite quick, about 2-3 taps per second.

backwards, stop tapping and scratch his wither. Your taps should be quite quick, about 2 - 3 per second. If you leave too much time between taps your horse might perceive it as a release of pressure, which is reinforcing. Keep practising until you can get a backwards step from either front leg.

If you leave too much time between your whip-taps your horse might perceive this as a release of pressure which could reinforce the wrong behaviour.

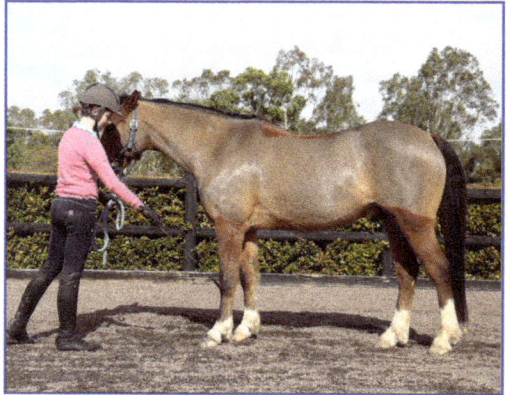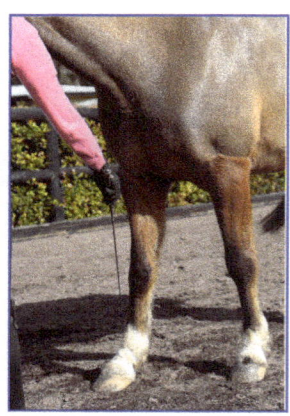

To make his response lighter, train him to step backwards from a whip tap on his cannon bone, just below his knee.

The next step is to apply a light signal with your reins first, before you tap his front leg. Your horse will very quickly learn that pressure on the reins is followed by tapping on his front legs and will start to step back from light rein pressure. He does this because of classical conditioning – just as Pavlov's dogs learned to drool when they heard the bell ring because they learned that the bell meant some meat was on its way.

Your horse will very quickly learn that pressure on the reins is followed by tapping.

Repeat this exercise, pairing rein pressure and front leg tapping, until your horse offers step back as soon as pressure is applied to the reins. You might notice that the pressure you need to use to achieve step back varies depending on which front leg is going to step back first. For example, your horse might be heavier when his left front leg is forward. If this is your horse, tap a little more quickly when the slower leg is forward and practise until he is even on both sides.

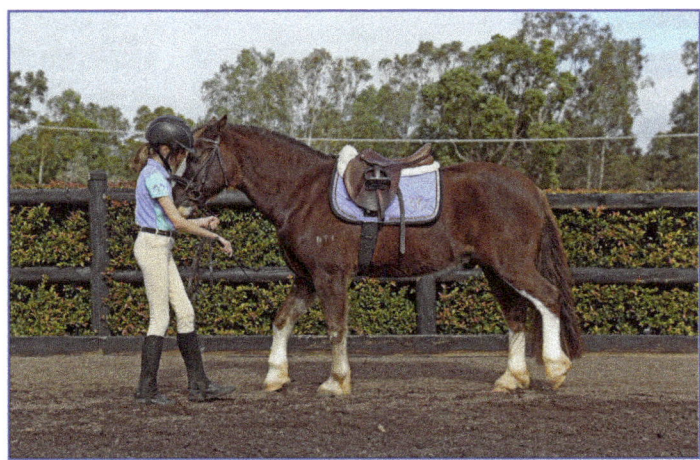

The next step is to apply a light signal with your reins first, before you tap his front leg. Your horse will very quickly learn that pressure on the reins is followed by tapping on his front legs and will start to step back from light rein pressure.

If your horse doesn't step backwards when you tap his cannon bone but instead offers some other response (like walking sideways) it's really important that you don't stop either the rein pressure or your tapping, but instead gradually increase the speed of your taps until he does step back. Using negative reinforcement is a little bit like going shopping for the correct behaviour. If you went to the supermarket to buy bread because you wanted a sandwich, you wouldn't buy a newspaper instead, even if that was the first item you came across as you walked into the shop. Rather, you'd keep shopping until you got to the section where the bread was kept because newspaper is not bread and tastes really bad in sandwiches. When you use negative reinforcement

Using negative reinforcement is a bit like shopping for the correct behaviour.

the first behaviour your horse chooses is not always the one you want. That's why it's so important to be precise when you stop applying pressure.

Once you've got light and immediate backward steps you can train your horse to offer two front leg steps backwards from a single signal. We like to call this the buy one, get one free game.

Once you have one light backward step, see if you can get two steps from one signal.

 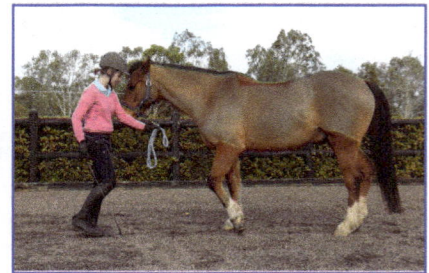

To achieve this, continue tapping during the step back of the first leg and don't stop until the other front leg begins to move backwards. Stop your tapping as soon as the second front leg begins to move backwards and offer lots of wither scratching straight afterwards too. Practise this until you can get two immediate backward steps from one signal.

If your horse gets anxious, you should go back to the most basic forms of the behaviour.

Nerd Word Alert!

A two leg step back is a good example of what we call shaping, which is just a fancy way of describing the gradual changing of behaviour through training. Shaping must be very gradual and if, at any stage, your horse becomes anxious or worried, you should go back to the most basic form of the behaviour and work through the shaping process again.

Once you have light backward steps you can add a voice cue. Most people use the word "back" but you can use whatever word you like because your horse can't speak English. Whatever word you use make sure you say it just before you use the rein cue for back. Always say it in exactly the same way and don't use it more than once every time. Remember the voice cue is, "back" and not, "Go back Rexy! I SAID BACK and I meant BACK... Oh for goodness sake go BACK you stupid animal!" Adding a single voice cue for each of the foundation responses increases the predictability of the environment for your horse (because of classical conditioning) and may make his responses even lighter.

When you have light backwards steps you can add a voice cue if you like.

When you can get two light backward steps from one signal you can make your horse's backward steps straight. You might have noticed that your horse rarely goes backwards in a perfectly straight line. This is because the legs of your horse work in diagonal pairs, that is, the left foreleg and the right hind leg work together and the right foreleg and the left hind leg work together. This occurs because of a nerve centre called the central pattern

The legs of your horse work in diagonal pairs - the left foreleg and right hind leg work together and the right foreleg and the left hind leg work together.

generator. The two diagonal pairs don't always work or move in the same way. If your horse is usually crooked in the step back it is quite likely that one of his diagonal pairs is less responsive to the stop signal than the other. You could think of that pair as being a bit of an under-achiever. If you are facing your horse and he swings his hindquarters to your left in the step back it is quite likely that the diagonal pair made up of his right front and left hind leg is not offering enough of a response to the stop signal. Funnily enough, the best way to fix this problem is to focus on training the front legs. This is because the way that the central pattern generator works means that the hind legs usually just copy what the front legs do.

Because of the central pattern generator, the hind legs usually just copy what the front legs do.

> ### A note on following...
> As we've already discussed, horses are extremely good at making connections between events. So, your horse quickly learns to move his legs backwards when you step towards him. Although it might seem harmless, we don't actually want the horse to follow our legs because there are lots of times when we don't want that to happen, for example when he's in the float, tied up or being ridden. Remember, we want the rules to be the same all the time so that your horse's life is as predictable as possible. Having unclear and inconsistent signals is the kind of surprise party that the horse doesn't like, so make sure that you always give your horse very light signals for go, stop and step back — don't allow him to just follow your legs.

It's best if you don't allow your horse to follow your legs, instead give clear signals for go and stop.

There are two ways that you can straighten your horse if he's crooked in the step back. You can tap his right front leg when it is in the air during a step back or you can apply a little more pressure on the rein when the right front leg is in the air during the step back. Either way, you are trying to get the under-achieving diagonal pair to work a little harder. (If your horse moves his quarters to your right you would target the left front leg.) If you have trouble coordinating your signals – don't worry, most people do at first. Just keep practising and you'll improve.

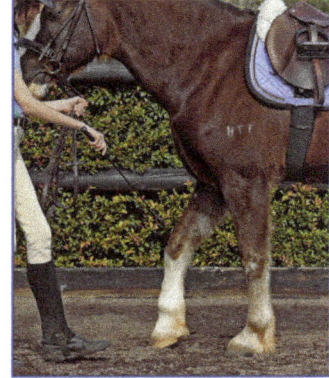

You can test your horse's straightness by asking him to do a step back between two parallel poles. Start with your poles at least one metre apart. If your horse can back quietly, from light signals between them, you can move them closer together. If you can do step backs between poles that are just a bit wider than your horse is, well done! Your horse is very straight.

If you have trouble coordinating your signals - don't worry, most people do at first. Just keep practising and you'll improve.

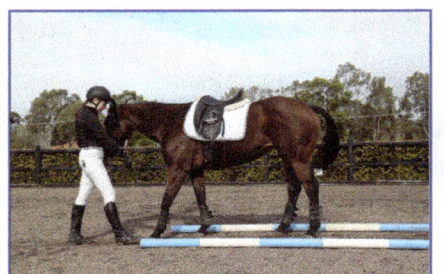 

You can test your horse's straightness by asking him to do a step back between two parallel poles.

Once you have mastered step back you can work on slow and stop. For this part of the exercise you are going to lead your horse in the usual way, standing on his left side with the reins in your right hand and the whip in your left.

You want your horse to stop in the time it takes him to do two steps with his front legs.

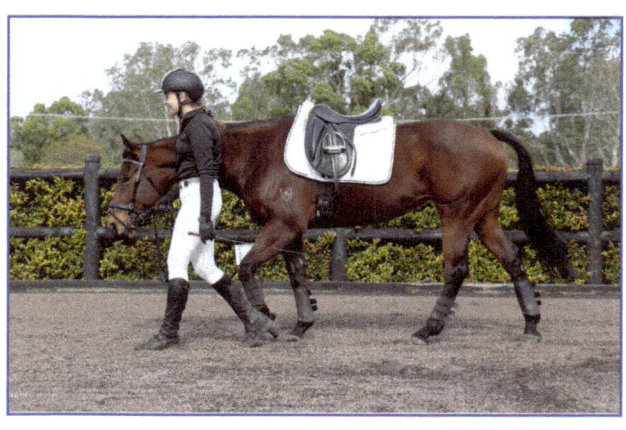

Ask your horse to walk forwards by applying a light pressure on the reins in the direction you want to go. Don't worry if your horse is heavy or sluggish in the upward transition, we'll fix that response soon. For now, we're focusing on stop and slow. Once he's walked a few strides, ask your horse to stop by applying pressure on the reins towards his wither (just as you did for step back). If he's heavy or delayed in his response you might have to vibrate the reins until he stops. If he's really heavy and delayed you can vibrate the reins and then tap his front legs as you did for step back. Don't forget to release the pressure as soon as he stops and give him a scratch and a stroke on his wither. You want him to stop in the time it takes him to do two steps with his front legs. Counting two front leg steps is a really good way of counting strides because in both walk and trot, two front leg steps means he's done a full stride.

Don't forget to release the pressure as soon as your horse stops and give him a scratch and a stroke on his wither.

Once you can get your horse to halt from a single, light signal you can practise making him walk really slowly, imagine that you are both walking on the moon. Your aim with this exercise is to get your horse to keep to whatever speed you want without being asked every stride. Release the pressure as he slows but be quick to reapply it if he speeds up – releasing every single time he slows, of course. You might have to repeat your cues every couple of strides in the beginning but if you're consistent and clear with your release, he'll soon get the idea. When a horse will maintain the same speed without either slowing down or speeding up on his own it is called self carriage. If you read some dressage books you might think that self carriage is something that happens around about Grand Prix level but it's something we should all strive for every day. Horses that aren't in self carriage are usually heavy in their responses and that's painful and causes them stress. Horses are very sensitive to pressure but they evolved to graze and hang out with their friends, not solve complex problems. It is our responsibility to train them well so that they will respond to light signals. Remember, we want chocolate bars, not lawnmowers.

You might have to repeat your cues every couple of strides in the beginning.

Horses are very sensitive to pressure but they evolved to graze and hang out with their friends, not solve complex problems.

When you are leading your horse you should practise making him walk where you want him to. Draw an imaginary line on the ground and don't let him veer away from it. It is quite common for horses to drift to the left while being led – which makes you feel as if they are going to step on your toes. If you can't correct this by using the rein to steer him to the right, do lots of downwards transitions, as quickening and drifting from your imaginary line often go together.

It helps to draw an imaginary line so you can tell if your horse is drifting left or right.

Practise making your horse walk where you want him to. It is quite common for horses to drift left while being led - which makes you feel as if they are going to step on your toes. Correct this by steering them to the right, or doing lots of downward transitions.

When your horse will walk at whatever speed you want, will halt lightly when being led and will take two steps backwards from one light signal, you can give yourself a big scratch on the wither because you've done a great job. You are well on the way to having an obedient and calm horse.

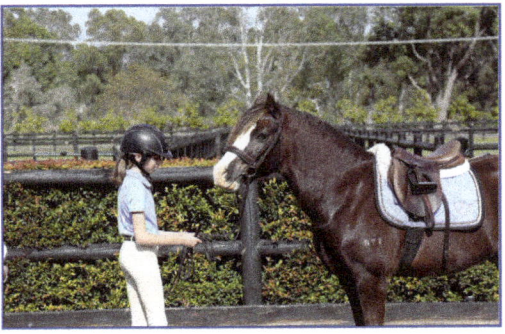

A note on space...
Some people think that you should train your horse to stay "out of your space" because they believe that when he steps close to you he is showing a lack of respect. It's a bit of a funny idea! If the horse is trained to stay a certain distance away from us at all times how are we going to put his saddle on or pick up his feet? How about riding? When you ride the horse you want to spend as much time as possible "in his space" – if you're not in his space you've probably fallen off! In reality, horses that walk too close to their handlers have not been trained to stop, slow and park correctly. Fixing these responses will ensure the handler can determine just how far away the horse is at all times.

When riding your horse, if you're not "in his space" you've probably fallen off!

Here's a place for you to write stuff!

Chapter Seven

Foundation responses in hand:
go forward and park

When we retrain problem behaviours (like bucking and shying) we always start with the stop and go forward responses in hand because, in our experience, horses with problem behaviours always have a failure with one and usually both of them. Therefore, the next foundation response that we're going to train is forwards. Our aim with this exercise is to get the horse to step forwards from light pressure on the reins.

Always ensure your horse is not frightened of the whip. It is a training aid, not a punishment tool.

> ### A note on space...
> If your horse is slow when you lead him, refuses to lead onto the float or into the wash bay, there's a very good chance that he has a problem with his go forwards response in hand.

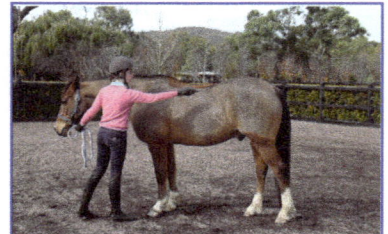
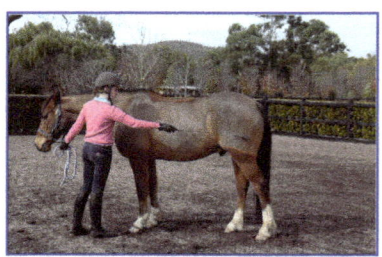

There is no correct amount of time for training, there is just the amount of time that it takes.

Begin by rubbing your horse gently all over with the whip to make sure that he isn't frightened of it. If he tries to step away from it, quietly step him backwards without moving the whip from his body.

Start by standing facing the horse's left shoulder with the reins in your left hand and the whip in your right. You are going to rub your horse gently all over with the whip to make sure that he isn't frightened of it. Start at his shoulder and move it gently all over his neck and rib cage. If he tries to step away from it, quietly step him backwards without removing the whip from his body. Negative reinforcement works even when you don't want it to, so if you take away the pressure of the whip when he moves, you can very quickly train him to move away from the whip. When he stands quietly you can take the whip away and give him lots of scratches as a reward. Make sure you can rub him with the whip on both sides of his body. This part of the training might take a couple of minutes or it might take many sessions over a few weeks. There is no correct amount of time, there is just the amount of time that it takes.

Negative reinforcement works even when you don't want it to, so if you take away the pressure of the whip when he moves, you can very quickly train him to move away from the whip.

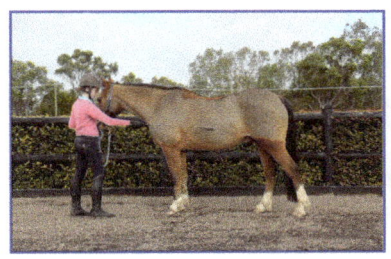 

If you can reach the round part of his ribcage easily with your whip you can tap there, otherwise you can tap the flat part of his shoulder.

For this exercise you are going to use light tapping as a cue to ask your horse to step forwards. If you can reach the round part of his ribcage easily with your whip you can tap there, otherwise you can tap the flat part of his shoulder, where the brand often is.

Apply a light pressure on the reins in the direction that you'd like him to step. If he doesn't move forwards straight away, maintain the pressure on the rein and also start tapping your whip very lightly on his ribcage. Increase the speed of your tapping until he takes a step forwards and immediately stop both rein and whip pressure. Reward him with lots of scratches and stroking. Practise this until you can get your horse to move forwards from just a light rein pressure and two light whip taps. You can add a voice cue for go now if you like. Some people use clicking or clucking, the choice is yours.

We all make lots of mistakes when learning new things, so it's ok if your horse doesn't get it right straight away, just keep asking until you get the behaviour you are after.

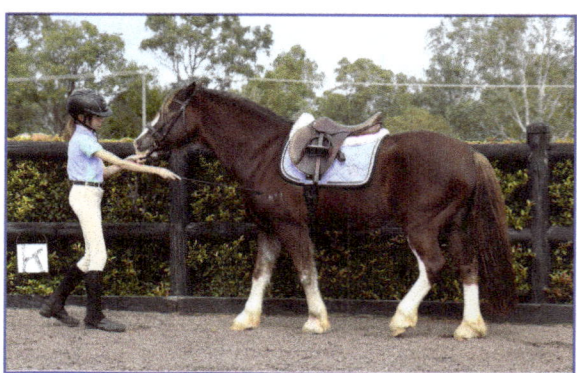

Apply light pressure on the rein in the direction that you'd like him to step. If he doesn't move forwards straight away, maintain the pressure on the rein and also start tapping your whip very lightly on his ribcage (or his shoulder if you can't reach his ribcage).

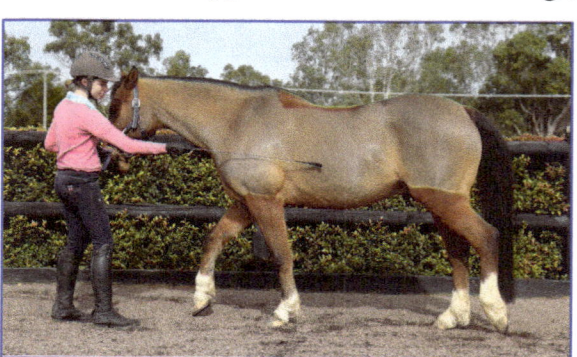

The gaps in your taps!

The whip taps you use in training must be mildly annoying, not painful. They need to be quick and consistent. To make your tapping more annoying, increase the speed of the taps, not the intensity. That is, don't make your taps harder, make them faster. If you have gaps between your taps of greater than a second, your horse might view this as a release of the pressure… which means it's reinforcing. Using your whip well takes practice. We recommend that you start practising on an annoying brother or sister.

If your horse moves sideways (instead of forwards) away from the tapping, don't panic and don't try to straighten him by changing your tapping to the other side. Just keep tapping and increase the pressure on the rein in a forward direction. When he takes a forward step, stop both pressures immediately and reward. Lots of horses will try to step sideways away from tapping during their initial training and that's ok because we all make lots and lots of mistakes when we're learning. When you were learning to feed yourself with a spoon you almost definitely spent a lot of time feeding the floor and the walls and your own hair – but you can probably use a spoon pretty well by now. Remember, you are going shopping for the right behaviour and that behaviour won't always be the first one that your horse offers.

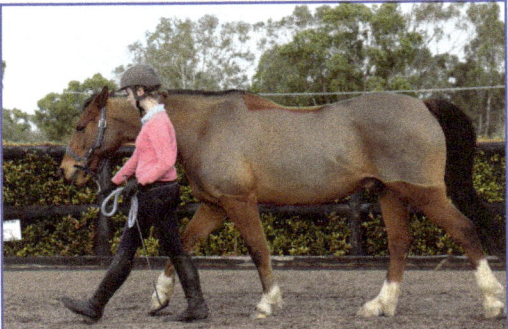

Remember, negative reinforcement is like shopping for the correct behaviour - and that behaviour won't always be the first one that your horse offers.

Remember, the whip is not to punish the horse, we are only using it to apply mildly annoying pressure to motivate him.

Now that you have light stop and go responses you can put them together and really test your horse's training. Lead your horse in the normal way – facing forwards with the reins in your right hand and the whip in your left. Practise doing really slow walk and really fast walk then alternate between the two. Practise the transitions between the gaits too: walk to trot, trot to walk and even trot to halt. You might find it hard to tap him with the whip at first but you'll soon improve if you practise. And remember, the whip is not to punish the horse or to hurt him, we are using it only to apply a mildly annoying pressure to motivate him.

When you can control your horse's legs with light signals, you are ready to train him outside the arena. Practise ground work wherever you can - just make sure you are always safe.

Practise your ground work wherever it is safe.

When you can control the speed of your horse's legs with light signals you are ready to train him outside the arena. Practise your ground work wherever it is safe. If your horse is not as obedient outside the arena as he is inside it, start off in the arena and introduce him to new areas very gradually.

The next thing that you can train your horse to do is park. A horse that has well established park doesn't move unless he's asked to. Park is a really important part of a horse's training because it shows us exactly what the horse knows about the stop and go responses. Park is really useful in many situations – when your horse is being shod, when you are rugging him, for mounting and when the vet comes. Park is also useful when training your horse to stay calm in new situations because he learns to wait for your signal to move.

> *Classically conditioned behaviours are like remote controlled toy cars. You have to keep charging them in order for them to work.*

To train park, draw an imaginary circle on the ground around your horse's legs. Stand facing him and gradually take a step backwards without pulling on the reins. If he steps forwards out of the imaginary circle, correct him by tapping his front legs (whichever if most forward) until he steps back into the circle.

To train park, draw an imaginary circle on the ground around your horse's legs. Stand facing him as you did in the early stop and go exercises. Take a step backwards without pulling on the reins. If he steps forwards out of the imaginary circle correct him by tapping his front legs until he steps back into the circle. If he steps backwards out of the imaginary circle, correct him by stepping him forwards. If he steps sideways out of the imaginary circle correct him by stepping him backwards then bringing him forwards back into the circle. Do this until you can step to the end of the reins without him following you and don't forget to give him lots of scratches when he gets it right.

Test park frequently and be sure to test it in lots of different areas.

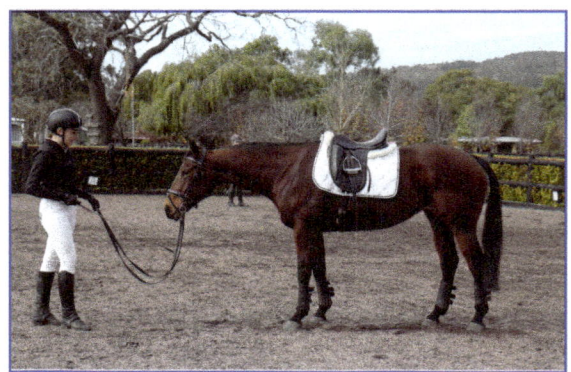

You can test park more by stepping to the left and right, and beginning to move away from your horse more quickly. Always increase the degree of difficulty very gradually so your horse is more likely to succeed.

Next, move to the end of the reins and take a couple of small steps to the left. Then take a few steps to the right. If he walks out of the circle, correct him as you did before. Keep practising until you can walk a little semi circle at the end of the reins — almost as if your horse was lunging you. Then move alongside your horse on his right side and walk forward, away from him. When this is easy, do it on his left hand side. This side will be harder because it's the side you lead him from and he's more used to following your legs, but just start with small steps and work gradually. Eventually you'll be able to run past your horse's shoulder (to the end of the reins) and he'll stand like a statue.

Eventually you'll be able to run around your horse and he'll stand like a statue.

When your horse can park in the arena you can test your training by asking him to park in other areas too. Start off in easy places like his stable or paddock and gradually increase the number of distractions. When you can park your horse in the warm up arena at a show or on the way home from a trail ride, you are definitely a ground work wizard!

You could design a ground work dressage test to further establish your horse's training. Perhaps you could have a competition with your friends or at your pony club. Keep in mind that if you can control your horse's legs he will be obedient but if you can control your horse's legs with light signals he will be obedient and calm. Your goal is to have a chocolate bar and not a lawnmower, regardless of distractions.

Your goal is to have a chocolate bar not a lawnmower, regardless of distractions.

When you can park your horse in the warm up arena at a show or on the way home from a trail ride, you are definitely a ground work wizard!

If your horse's foundation responses are not perfect in a distracting situation consider it a firewall.

Overshadowing can be hard to overcome, but it can also be a useful training tool.

What is overshadowing?

If your horse is really hard to control when things distract him it is because he is overshadowed by the environment. Overshadowing happens because horses can't do two things at once. So, you might find it really difficult to control your horse on a very windy day or when there are lots of other horses around because he can't focus on both the distractions and your signals at the same time. You might find that you have to increase the pressure of your signals in order to get him to respond. That's ok. Don't punish him or change your training. If your horse's foundation responses are not perfect in a distracting situation consider that a firewall. In training, a firewall, like the virus protection software on your computer, stops you from going on when things aren't right. Don't try anything more complicated (like jumping) until your horse's responses are light and obedient. Do lots and lots of repetitions of the foundation responses and eventually, he will habituate to the distractions.

Overshadowing can be a useful tool to help your horse habituate to scary things like clippers. You can step him forwards and backwards while someone approaches him with clippers (start with them turned off). When his normally light responses become heavy, get your assistant to stop their approach while you keep stepping him forwards and backwards until he is light again. Your assistant can then continue approaching. Every time your horse gets heavy get your assistant to stop and don't ask her to start again until he is light. Then start the process over with the clippers turned on.

Chapter Eight

Foundation responses under saddle: stop

Now that both you and your horse have mastered ground work you can start the really fun stuff – training under saddle. In this book we are going to cover the basic foundation responses that all horses need under saddle. It doesn't matter what you do with your horse, if you ride him he needs to be able to stop, go and turn from light signals or his ridden life is going to be full of surprise parties.

Your horse needs to stop, go and turn from light signals or his ridden life is going to be full of surprise parties.

Before we begin.... You don't need a lot of fancy equipment to train a horse well but you do need to be safe. You will need an enclosed area to ride in. It doesn't have to be an arena but you do need somewhere that is relatively flat with a surface that isn't slippery. Ideally your working area should be large enough for your horse to canter around safely.

You can use any kind of saddle you like as long as it fits your horse well, is in good and safe condition, and is comfortable for you. A simple, snaffle bridle is best for training. If you use a noseband, regardless of what type, you need to be able to get two fingers comfortably between the noseband and your horse. Tight

Tight nosebands are uncomfortable for the horse and can affect his breathing.

nosebands are uncomfortable for your horse and can affect his breathing. Some people think that doing the noseband up really tight will help them stop their horse but it's far kinder to train and maintain the stop response than cause the horse pain with a tight noseband. You would find it uncomfortable if your mouth was tied shut while you were at school and I'm sure your horse doesn't like it much either – although if it stopped you from talking in class your teacher might think it was quite a good idea…

Fitting your noseband…

If you use a noseband, regardless of what type, you need to be abe to get two fingers comfortably between the noseband and your horse. Tight nosebands are uncomfortable for your horse and can affect his breathing and his ability to swallow. Tightening the noseband to close the horse's mouth or give the rider more control is just covering up mistakes in the training and won't make your horse's life better.

Remember, of all the things that you could lose, you'd miss your mind the most. Always wear a helmet when handling or riding your horse.

You will need a properly fitted helmet. Remember, of all the things that you could lose you'd miss your mind the most – so you need to look after your head and what's inside it! Riding boots are also a necessity as they are designed to come free from the stirrup if you fall. Speaking of safety… horse riding is a dangerous sport and before you mount your horse you should ask yourself if you have the necessary experience and skills to do it properly. If you're not sure, some lessons at a local riding school should improve your skills and help to keep you safe. Ideally you would work through the exercises in this book with the help of an instructor or an experienced person.

> *Postural changes in the horse's head and neck should develop as a result of correct basic training and shouldn't be seen as the goal of training.*

You might have noticed that the foundation responses we will be working on are all aimed at controlling the legs of the horse and do not include anything that changes the position of the neck and head. Postural changes in the horse's head and neck should develop as a result of correct basic training and shouldn't be seen as the goal of training. When a horse is "on the bit" not only is his neck a little bit arched (how much depends on the level of his training) but he is also relaxed, loose through his body and attentive to the signals from his rider. In some ways, the arched neck is a little bit like icing on a cake. You can make a horse with incorrect training assume the "on the bit" position, but it is like putting icing on a half baked or mouldy cake – it will soon become obvious that the cake is not good, despite the icing. In this book we deal only with the foundation responses and jumping. During this training, the horse does not have to be 'on the bit'.

> *Focus on keeping a steady, even contact on the reins with just enough pressure to keep the reins from having a loop in them.*

During the training of the foundation responses, your horse does not have to be 'on the bit'.

When you ride your horse you should focus on keeping a steady, even contact on the reins. When you have a contact it should only be as much pressure as is needed to keep the reins straight, just enough pressure to stop them from flapping and sagging while you ride. This way the rein signals you use can be really light because you only have to move your fingers and your horse will feel it. If you have reins that dangle, every time you want to send a signal to your horse you need to take up the slack and then apply the signal. It's like having a phone conversation where you have to redial the phone every time you want to speak. If you have tight reins all the time it is as though you are constantly giving the signal for stop. This is very uncomfortable for the horse and bad for your training.

If you have tight reins all the time it is as though you are constantly giving the signal for stop. This is very uncomfortable for the horse and bad for your training.

You should aim to have a light, steady contact on the reins when you are riding your horse (left). If you have reins that dangle (right), it takes longer to apply each signal.

Did you know?
Problems with the stop response can show up as rushing, tension, jogging, reefing on the reins, heaviness in the downward transitions, spooking, spinning, bucking or bolting. Dangerous problem behaviours like bucking or bolting require the assistance of a professional trainer.

Beginning with some ground work before each ridden session helps to check your horse's responses and keep you safe.

You can begin each ridden session with some ground work to check your horse's responses are working well. Always do some ground work before you mount if you are riding in a new area.

You can begin each ridden session with some ground work. Make sure you can stop, go and park before you mount. This will ensure your horse is calm and ready to progress to the next stage of training. If your horse moves off while you are mounting make sure you have really reliable park in hand next to the mounting block. You need to train your horse to stand still while being mounted because if he moves off without being asked it is a little bit of a surprise party. Mount with the reins in your left hand and if, at any time, your horse starts to move, correct him by applying pressure on the reins. You need to train your horse to wait for your cue before he walks forwards.

Training your horse to park at the mounting block will make life easier for you both!

You need to train your horse to park for you to mount.

We are going to begin with the stop response. Once you have mounted your horse ask him to walk forwards. Ride a downward transition to halt by applying pressure on the reins. Just use the reins only – don't use your legs at the same time because that's confusing for the horse and not necessary. Remember, your horse can't multi task so only ever give one signal at a time. You are using negative reinforcement which means you'll start with very light pressure and increase it until your horse stops. As soon as he stops your pressure should return to being only just enough to keep your reins straight.

Just use your reins for stopping and slowing down - don't use your legs at the same time because that's confusing for the horse and not necessary.

Begin by riding a downward transition from walk to halt. You're using negative reinforcement which means you'll start with very light pressure and increase it until your horse stops (left). As soon as he stops, your pressure should return to being only just enough to keep your reins straight (right).

Now do another halt and this time count how many steps your horse takes with his front legs during the transition. This part takes some practice and it might be useful to have someone on the ground to help you count. How many front leg steps did your horse take to stop? Ideally we want the horse to stop in one stride – that means just two front leg steps. If you have trouble getting your halt in a stride you might have to increase the pressure a little bit more quickly. That's ok, as long as you always begin with very light pressure. Don't forget to stroke or scratch your horse when he gets it right.

Give your horse a stroke or scratch frequently during training.

Doing three sets of four to five repetitions of each behaviour helps the horse to learn quickly without stress.

A really effective way to train your horse is to do three sets of four to five repetitions of each behaviour. So, if you are training halts you can do four or five halts in a row. Then give your horse some time off – go for a walk around the arena, stand in the shade and relax or work on something else. Then do another four or five repetitions with another little rest and then another four or five repetitions. In this way you will have done three sets of four or five repetitions. This method helps horses learn quickly without stress.

Riding four or five repetitions of each exercise helps the horse to learn quickly without stress. You can also practise doing a step backwards under saddle to help strengthen your horse's stop response.

You can also practise doing step back under saddle because this will help strengthen your horse's stop response. When your horse is halted, close your fingers on the reins and apply pressure in the same way that you would in a downward transition. Release the pressure as soon as your horse starts to take a backward step. Don't try this exercise until your horse has a light and obedient step back response on the ground.

> *Practising backwards steps is a great way to strengthen your horse's stop response.*

Playing the counting game is a great way to make sure your horse's stop response is even and light.

A good way to practise getting your horse's stop response really clear is to play a counting game. Starting in halt, walk your horse forward for six steps of his front legs and then ride a downward transition to halt. You could get a friend to help you from the ground if you're having trouble counting. Keep doing six steps of walk then halt, six steps of walk, halt. If you can do six steps (not seven or five with a shuffle) your horse will stop with alternating front legs and start with alternating front legs. So, it's a great way to make sure that his halts are even on both sides.

> *Play the counting game to make sure your horse's halts are even on both sides.*

> **To get your downward transitions in one stride (two front leg steps), you need to do the transition in the time it takes you to go sit-rise-sit.**

When you can stop your horse in one stride from a light signal you can practise your downward transitions from trot. Eventually you'd like to be able to achieve these transitions in one stride as well. If you are in rising (or posting) trot it's easy to count one stride because it occurs in the time it takes you to rise and sit. So, if you start your downward transition as you sit, your horse should be walking by the time you've gone rise-sit once more. These transitions take a bit more practice because everything happens more quickly at trot.

When rising (or posting) to the trot, it's easy to count one stride because it occurs in the time it takes you to rise and sit.

> **Trot to halt transitions are harder because you have to go down two gears, not just one.**

Once you can do trot to walk transitions in one stride and from a light signal, you can try trot to halt transitions. These are a little bit harder because your horse will have to go down two gears, instead of just one. It helps if you close your fingers quite firmly on the reins and put your elbows by your sides – don't flap your arms around like a bird flying! Aim to have your horse go from trot to halt in two strides, that's four steps of his front legs. As your horse's training progresses you can shape that response so that he stops in three steps of his front legs and eventually, if your training is very clear, you should be able to stop him with a light signal in two steps of his front legs.

Eventually, if your training is very clear, you should be able to stop your horse with a light signal in two steps of his front legs.

You don't have to do trot to halt transitions every time you train your horse but it is very useful to practise them before you do any jumping because sometimes even well trained horses can show the flight response while jumping and it's very good to brush up on your stopping and slowing down skills before you start.

Don't always practise your halts against the fence. Make sure you can do them anywhere. This way you'll test your horse's straightness too!

Don't always practise your halts against the fence, make sure you can do them anywhere. If your horse swerves during the downward transition (even a little bit) it is usually because one of his diagonal pairs of legs is not stopping as well as the other. To train him to remain straight, during the downward transition use a little bit more rein on the side of the front leg that doesn't stop as well. For example, if your horse drifts to the left in the downward transition try riding the downward transition with a

Don't try to keep your horse straight in the downward transition by using your legs. It would be like telling your horse to stop and go at the same time which is impossible!

little bit more pressure in your left rein – you are asking all the legs to stop but asking the left front/right hind pair to stop a little bit more. Don't try to keep him straight with your legs as it would be like telling him to go and stop at the same time, and that's impossible!

Once you can stop your horse immediately from a light signal you are ready to train him to slow. If your horse has trouble with going forwards, you might have to skip this stage and go straight to the next chapter. Don't worry you can come back and train him to slow later.

In a rock band it is the drummer who is responsible for telling all the other musicians what tempo they should play and sing in. When you ride your horse you are like the drummer because you decide on the speed of your horse's legs. Tempo is very

Tempo is very important for recognising and eliminating flight response during training.

important when you train your horse because any quickening could be an expression of the flight response – which we definitely do not want. Slowing is also a problem and can cause baulking and even rearing if

it isn't corrected. When drummers are practising they sometimes use a device called a metronome to help them keep the right tempo. Metronomes make a beeping sound in a set speed and they can be very useful for horse riders too – you can buy them in music shops or download an electronic one for your smartphone.

The tempo of your horse's legs will change as he changes gaits. If he is over 14.2hh he will usually walk at about 55 beats per minute (bpm) – which means that one of his front legs will touch the ground 55 times per minute. He will usually trot at approximately

Tempo refers to the speed of the footfalls and rhythm is the regularity of the footfalls.

If your horse is over 14.2hh he will usually walk at about 55 beats per minute (bpm), trot at 75bpm and canter at 95bpm.

Nerd word alert...
Although they are often confused, when we talk about horse training, rhythm and tempo are two separate things. Tempo refers to the speed of the footfalls and rhythm is the regularity of the footfalls. If you can control the tempo of your horse you can control his speed. If you can maintain the rhythm, your horse is not slowing down or speeding up.

Think of the correct tempo as the Goldilocks tempo - it's not too fast and not too slow, it's just right!

75bpm and canter at about 95bpm. Ponies can be about 5 beats per minute quicker than that in all three gaits. We sometimes call the right tempo the Goldilocks tempo because it's not too fast and not too slow, it's just right!

Riding to the beats of the metronome can be quite tricky at first but you'll find it really useful once you get better at it.

Set your metronome to 55bpm and try to walk your horse at that speed. It might help if you watch one of his shoulders or ask a friend to help you out from the ground. It can be quite tricky, but if you practise you'll soon master it. When you are happy that you can ride your horse at 55bpm, change your metronome and ride your horse at 50bpm and then at 60bpm. If you have someone on the ground to work the metronome you can practise swapping between the three speeds. It takes quite a lot of concentration but it really helps train your horse to be obedient to the slowing signals.

Once you have good control of the tempo at the walk you can set your metronome to 75bpm and try it at the trot. It can be very exciting at first for some horses to go faster than 75bpm in the trot, so stick to 75 and slower until you feel confident that you have control.

It's important that your horse learns to maintain the tempo on his own.

Testing the self-carriage in the trot. This is a very important exercise to develop calmness and test your horses' foundation responses.

One of the best exercises you can do to develop calmness and self carriage is slow trot. See if you can ride your horse at 70bpm. It's important that he learns to maintain the tempo on his own, so don't keep a constant pressure on the reins but use them to slow him every time he quickens and then release the pressure when he slows. You might have to slow him every couple of strides at first but eventually he'll learn to keep to the tempo that you decide on. Remember, you're the drummer in this band! Once you can do 70bpm comfortably, see if you can go slower. Some horses seem to be able to maintain a very slow tempo while others find it harder. Your goal is to be able to maintain a tempo slower than 70bpm for several laps of your working area.

You can use slow trot any time you think your horse might be showing the flight response.

You can use your slow trot any time you think your horse might be showing the flight response. Park in hand and slow trot under saddle are two of the best exercises you can do in situations that might make your horse excited because you can be very clear about the way you control his legs which allows you to prevent or limit any flight response.

Slow trot is helping this horse to master self-carriage. You can see how relaxed she is by her natural head carriage and soft expression.

Chapter Nine

Foundation responses under saddle: go forwards

The next foundation response that we're going to train is go forwards. The signal for go is pressure from both lower legs at the same time. Make sure when you ask your horse to go forwards that you have only enough pressure on your reins to keep them straight. Any more than that and you are asking for stop and go at the same time and that's impossible for your horse. As soon as your horse moves forward, release the pressure from your legs.

The signal for go forward is pressure from both lower legs at the same time.

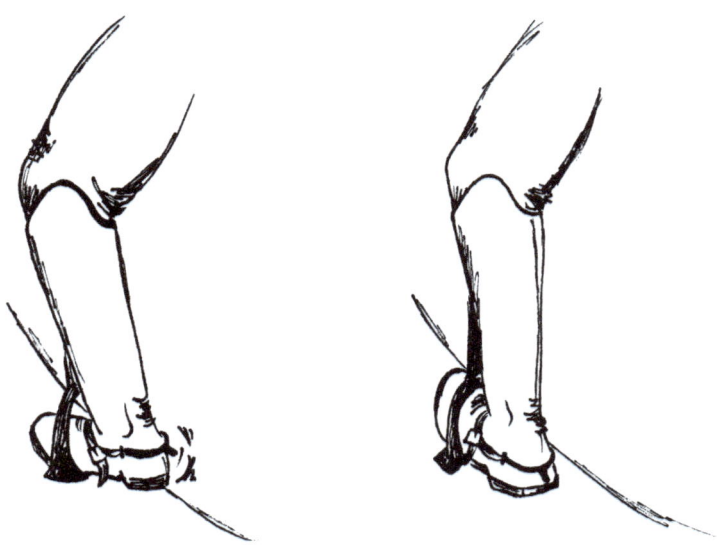

The signal for go forward is pressure from both lower legs at the same time. Remember that the release of the pressure (right) is the most important part of the aid, or signal. Note: you shouldn't need to wear spurs to get your horse to go forwards.

You shouldn't need to wear spurs to get your horse to go forwards.

If your horse is slow to go, requires a strong leg signal or slows immediately without being asked, you will probably need to retrain his go responses and for this process you will need your whip. Before you started your under saddle training, you trained your horse to step forwards on the ground from two light whip taps. If you tapped his ribcage for go on the ground you'll use the ribcage for go under saddle. If you tapped the shoulder for go on the ground you'll use the shoulder under saddle. You've already started training these responses, so it will make achieving them under saddle easier if you stick to the same place. Once your horse is really clear about the go forwards signal you can transfer your tapping to wherever is easiest for you to reach.

Did you know?
Problems with the go forwards response often show up as behaviours like baulking at jumps, refusing to go, jibbing or rearing. Dangerous problem behaviours like rearing require the assistance of a professional trainer.

Problems with the go forwards response often show up as behaviours like baulking at jumps, refusing to go and napping towards home.

You are going to begin the retraining process by training your horse to go forwards from light tapping of the whip only – no leg signals at all. Once he can do this reliably you'll then reintroduce your leg signals. This process can be a little bit exciting for some horses so it's important that you have someone knowledgeble to supervise you. Your horse must also be  REALLY clear and reliable with his go response on the ground. If you can't achieve immediate upwards transitions from light signals on the ground, go back to your groundwork and practise until it's as close to perfect as you can make it.

If you are right handed you probably taught your horse to go forward on the ground by tapping him on his left side or shoulder. So begin with the whip in your left hand. Start by tapping lightly on his side, increasing the speed of the taps until he takes a step forwards – and then stop tapping. Remember, using negative reinforcement is a little bit like shopping, you've got to keep shopping until you get what you want... so don't stop your pressure until you get a forward step.

Remember, using negative reinforcement is a bit like shopping, you've got to keep going until you get what you want... so don't stop your pressure until you get a forward step.

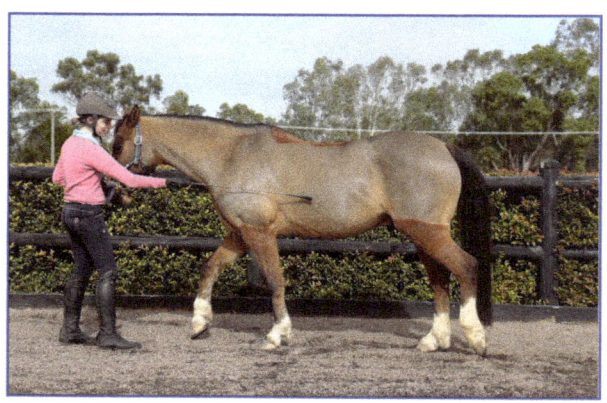

If you are right handed you probably taught your horse to go forward by tapping him on his left side or shoulder. This means you'll need to begin your under saddle training using the whip in your left hand so you can tap the same spot.

If your horse takes a very small step forwards you should stop tapping and reward him with a stroke on his neck. It's important that you reward every single 'good try' that your horse makes. Take your time and don't try to hurry. Although it might seem simple to you, for your horse it might be as difficult as it was for you to learn long division or to speak another language.

For your horse, new behaviours are as difficult as learning long division, or a foreign language.

But what about the seat?

When horses don't go or stop, people will often suggest that the rider should use their seat to fix it. And while it is true that in a really well trained horse the seat gives signals about changes in tempo, the most reliable training involves negative reinforcement.

Remember Pavlov? Just as Pavlov's bell let his dogs know that their meat was coming, so too do changes in the rider's seat let the horse know that leg or rein signals are coming. However, on its own Pavlov's bell would have had no effect on his dogs. And the same is true of the seat signals – they only work because they are associated (because of classical conditioning) with rein and leg cues. This means they can't be used to fix problems in the foundation responses – that's the job of negative reinforcement.

While classical conditioning is often a useful tool for the horse trainer, the most reliable training involves negative reinforcement.

Once you can do halt to walk transitions with whip taps only, you can train walk to trot transitions. Use your whip taps to ask your horse to walk and, once he's walking, use whip taps to get him to trot. Remember, you're not using any leg at all for this exercise, just your whip. Not all horses will go forwards from whip taps immediately under saddle. The better trained your horse is on the ground, the more likely it is that the retraining process under saddle will be straight forward. If your horse offers some alternatives to forward such as kicking out or moving sideways, it's important not to stop tapping until he goes forward. If, however, he offers dangerous alternatives such as leaping or bucking you should get some help from an experienced trainer.

> *The better trained your horse is on the round, the more likely it is that the retraining process under saddle will be straight forward.*

With repetition and practice you should be able to get your horse from halt to walk, and from walk to trot with just two light whip taps.

With repetition and practice you should be able to get your horse from halt to walk and from walk to trot with just two light whip taps. Once he will go forward from whip taps on his left side, repeat the process with the whip on the right.

Once you've mastered go forwards from the whip, you can train your horse to respond to your leg. Apply light leg pressure and, while you're still pressing with your leg, introduce the light whip taps. As soon as your horse goes forward remember to release both your legs and stop the tapping.

Because of classical conditioning, your horse will learn that the pressure of your legs is followed by the annoying whip tap - so he'll choose to go forwards from the light leg pressure to avoid the tapping.

Once you have mastered go forwards from the whip you can train your horse to respond to your leg. You're going to do this with classical conditioning. So, apply a light leg aid and, while you're still pressing your horse with your leg, introduce the light whip taps that you used before. When he goes forwards you'll release both pressures and scratch his neck. This part of the training should be pretty straight forward if you've done the previous part thoroughly. Pretty soon your horse will learn that the mild pressure of your leg is followed by the annoying whip taps – so he chooses to go forward from a light leg pressure.

Once you can do halt to walk transitions with just a light leg signal you can move onto walk to trot transitions. You can also use your light signal to ask your horse to increase the speed of his legs in the walk and the trot (and eventually in the canter too). You should be able to do all your upward transitions from just a light leg signal. If your horse's responses become dull you can quickly remind him of his training by going back to using whip taps for a few transitions.

If your horse's responses become dull again you can quickly remind him of his training by going back to using whip taps for a few repetitions.

Once your horse is light and obedient in the upward transitions you can train him to stay at the same tempo.

Once your horse is light and obedient in the upward transitions you can train him to stay at the same tempo. Some horses are always slowing down – these horses are often called "lazy" but really it's just a little gap in their training. They need to be trained to maintain the tempo of their legs until the rider tells them otherwise. If your horse slows when he is walking or trotting it can be quite tempting to keep nudging him with your leg to keep him in your tempo, kind of like pedalling a bike. The

Remember that your leg aid should always mean "go forwards", not just "keep going".

problem with this approach is that your leg should always mean "go forward", it shouldn't ever mean "keep going". That is, your leg should always quicken your horse's legs not keep them in the same tempo.

If your horse slows in the walk, do an upward transition to trot and then, after a few strides, ride a downward transition to walk again. Don't pedal! Make sure you only use your leg for going forwards. It's almost as if you are daring your horse to slow down and when he does, you correct him by riding an upward transition. If you're careful about not using your leg for anything other than go forward, pretty soon your horse will realise that it's much easier to maintain his own tempo. Just remember that you are the drummer in this band and you decide on the speed of your horse's legs.

If your horse slows down in the walk, do an upward transition to trot and then, after a few strides, ride a downward transition to walk again.

When you can do light upward transitions from your leg in walk and trot you can also do trot to canter transitions.

When you can do light upward transitions from your leg in walk and trot you can also do trot to canter transitions as well. In the canter there is an instant in each stride (called the moment of

111

The moment of suspension.

It is very important to have soft, elastic elbows in the canter so that you can move your hands forwards and backwards as the horse rocks his head up and down.

suspension) when all the horse's legs are off the ground. Your horse's head rocks up and down in the canter – a little bit like a bird pecking at seed. This is why you must have really elastic elbows, so you can keep a light contact on the reins without jerking them every stride. (This is true at the walk as well, but the movement of his head in the walk is much slower and therefore easier to follow.) In the canter, when your horse's head is at the highest point, he is in the moment of suspension. This is the best time to slow or quicken because all his legs are off the ground.

Test your self-carriage frequently. You want to be sure that your horse doesn't speed up or slow down unless you ask him to.

Chapter Ten

Foundation responses
under saddle: turn

There are two types of turn under saddle - direct turn, and indirect turn.

There are two kinds of turn under saddle – direct and indirect. Because of this and because it's not always easy to tell if a turn is correct or not, turn is the most complex of the foundation responses. We're going to start with direct turn because this is the kind you'll use most often. However, in order to really understand turn you'll first need to know a little bit about biomechanics, which is the study of how living things move. Have you ever wondered why your horse's legs never get tangled? If you've ever taken dancing lessons you'll know that it's hard enough to control two legs, let alone four! Yet the horse seems to do it easily. This is because of a special bunch of nerves called the central pattern generator. The central pattern generator links the horse's legs together in diagonal pairs. That means that the left front leg and the right hind leg are linked, while the right front leg and the left hind leg are linked. The front legs of the horse are the easiest to control, which is why in training we usually focus on them.

The central pattern generator links the horse's legs together in diagonal pairs.

Now, here's where it gets a bit weird... Each diagonal pair of legs acts a little bit differently, and you've probably already discovered this for yourself. Remember when you were teaching your horse to step backwards, it was difficult in the beginning to make him go backwards in a straight line? This is because one of his diagonal pairs was a bit of an underachiever. You tapped a little more on one front leg to correct it and this made him straight. When you're training turn responses you'll probably discover that your horse turns well in one direction, but not so well in the other. This is not because he likes one way better than the other but because the central pattern generator makes his leg pairs work a little bit differently to each other.

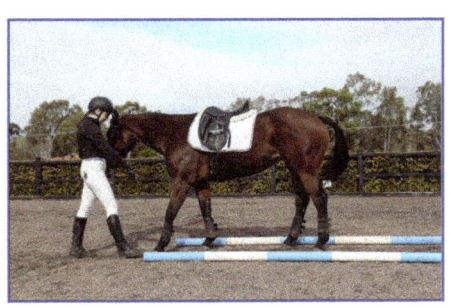

> *You'll probably find your horse turns better in one direction than the other. This isn't because he likes one way better than the other but because the central pattern generator makes his leg pairs work a little bit differently to each other.*

When your horse is moving, his legs are either in the air or on the ground. When they're in the air they are in the swing phase. When they're on the ground they're in the stance phase. Although it sounds strange, the horse's legs are controlled by different parts of the brain, depending on what phase they're in. The easiest time to send a signal to the legs is when they're in the swing phase – particularly when they are moving forwards.

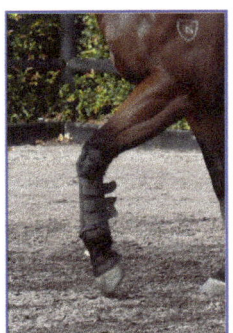 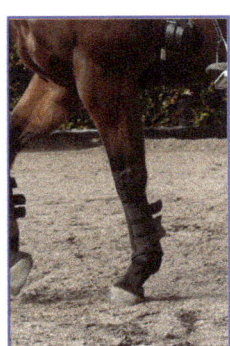

Swing phase. *Stance phase.*

> *The easiest time to send a signal to the legs is when they're in the swing phase.*

Direct Turn

When your horse's legs are in the swing phase, as well as moving straight they can abduct (move away from his body) or adduct (move towards his body). When your horse does a correct turn to the left, his left front leg abducts while it is in the swing phase. That is, it moves away from his body while it is in the air. That's the first step. The second step is the right front leg adducting during the swing phase.

The best way to understand turn is to get down on your hands and knees and do it yourself.

When your horse does a correct turn to the left, his left front leg abducts (moves away from his body) while it is in the swing phase (left). The second step of the turn is the right front leg adducting during the swing phase (right).

The best way to understand turn is to get down on your hands and knees and do it yourself. Crawl forwards on the floor and then make a sharp turn to the left. In the first step of turn your left arm (which you're going to pretend is your left front leg) moves away from your body. In the second step of the turn your right arm/right front leg moves towards your body. Right turn works the same, but it is the right front leg that abducts in the first step and so on.

It always helps to look the way you are turning - mostly because it helps you to avoid crashing into things! Use an opening rein (away from the horse's neck) for the direct turn aid.

> *Your horse's neck should make a very gentle arc - not a right angle or a banana.*

When you give your horse the pressure cue to turn left at the walk you're first going to look to the left. This bit is pretty important because otherwise you might crash into things. Then, by moving your hand slightly away from the horse's neck, you apply pressure on the left rein. We call this an opening rein. Your right hand stays in its usual position on the right side of your horse's neck and keeps enough tension on the rein to prevent his neck from bending too much. In a correct direct turn response the horse will bend his neck very slightly in the direction that he is going. His neck should make a very gentle arc – not a right angle or a banana. Don't pull his nose out past the point of his inside shoulder because this can unbalance him. It is the job of the outside rein to manage the bend of the neck in the turn.

> *Don't pull your horse's nose out past the point of his shoulder because this can unbalance him. It is the job of the outside rein to manage the bend of the neck in the turn.*

Did you know?
Problems with the turn response might show up as running out when jumping, shying, spinning, falling in, falling out and jibbing. Dangerous problem behaviours like spinning require the assistance of a professional trainer.

The pressure cue for turn is always an opening rein, never a pulling backwards rein.

If your horse doesn't have very clear turn reponses you might have to begin his training by opening your rein quite a lot, but gradually over time that cue can be made smaller until, eventually, just a little bit of pressure on the turning rein will produce a turn response. Remember, the pressure cue for turn is always an opening rein, never a pulling backwards rein – which often just encourages the horse to bend his neck. Riders generally find it easier to pull backwards on the rein because the bicep muscle in your arm (the one that body builders are always showing off) is generally stronger than your tricep muscle. And it's the tricep muscle that produces an opening rein.

If your horse doesn't have very clear turn responses you might have to begin his training by opening your rein quite a lot, but gradually over time that cue can be made smaller. Be sure to keep his neck from bending too much in the turn.

Never do sharp turns on horses because they can slip over - this is particularly true in the canter.

Canter tips...

In the canter it's easy to tell when your horse's inside front leg is in the swing phase. This occurs during the moment of suspension – when your horse's head is at its highest point within the stride. You should never do sharp turns on horses because they might slip over and this is particularly true in the canter.

A correct turn response does not need any leg cues.

The other thing that it's important to understand is that a correct turn response does not need any leg cues. This is very important. Leg cues are unnecessary in turn and usually only end up making the go forwards response less clear. Think back to the ten principles of training – we should only ever use one cue at a time. Your horse learns to turn from really light signals because when you look in the direction that you are going to turn, it changes the way your body sits in the saddle and he soon learns to associate this feeling with the turn response. How does this occur? If you said classical conditioning you are completely correct!

> *It is important to understand that a correct turn response does not need any leg cues.*

You're going to practise your direct rein turns at walk first because it's easier to see what is going on when your horse is walking. You will need some marker cones so you can ride accurate lines. You can buy cones from your local saddlery or sports store but if you don't have them you can use anything that is smooth and won't hurt your horse if he treads on or kicks it.

> *Always practise at walk first. Marker cones will be useful for your training so you can be sure to ride accurate lines.*

Initially you might need two turn signals to get around each of the corners.

Start by using four cones to mark out a square with sides of about 15m. Ride around the square using direct turn. It's usually harder than it sounds.

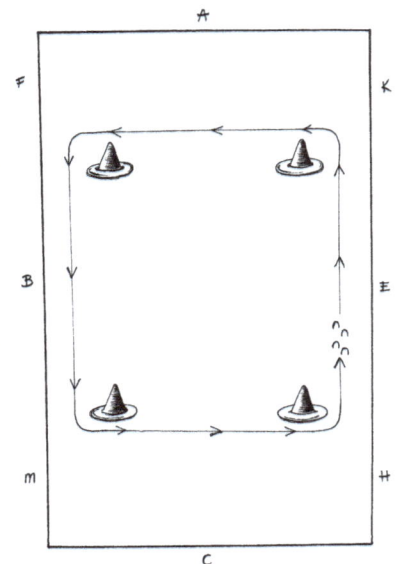

You are going to apply your turn signal while your horse's inside leg is in the swing phase. In the beginning you can look down at the inside shoulder to work out when that is. You should release your turn signal once your horse's inside front leg has moved away from his body during the step. In the beginning you might need two turn signals to get around each of the corners of your square, but, like the buy one, get one free game you played with your horse on the ground, you will soon be able to turn the corners from one signal.

It is important that your horse maintains the same tempo as he turns. That is, he doesn't speed up or slow down when you ride a turn.

A note on circles...
A circle is actually quite an advanced turn exercise because it requires the horse to do a little bit of turn with every step. That's why good trainers often ride circles on young horses as a series of many small turns. Their circles might look a bit like hexagons but their horses' turn responses are clear!

Once you can turn your horse around each of the corners of the square with just one light signal on both reins, you're going to get your metronome. Set it to 55 beats per minute and repeat the exercise. Does your horse's rhythm change in the turn? If he speeds up around the corner you're going to slow his tempo just before and just after the turn. If he slows down, you'll quicken him just before and just after the turn. You won't try to change his tempo during the turn because that would be applying two signals at once. Once you have mastered turn at 55bpm try it at 50bpm and 60bpm. This phase of your horse's training might happen in a single training session or it might take several sessions. Don't give up or skip ahead because you're going to need those good turn responses once you start jumping.

> **Training your horse's turn responses may take a single training session or it might take several sessions. Don't give up or skip ahead because you're going to need those good turn responses once you start jumping.**

Turns at trot are much harder because everything happens faster so it's more difficult to know when the turning leg is in the swing phase.

When you have really reliable turn responses at walk you can move onto training the turn at trot. This is much harder because everything happens faster so it's more difficult to know when the turning leg is in the swing phase. You're going to start with small turns at trot by riding shallow loops in both directions – a wiggly line all the way around your working area. This exercise is both a training tool and a way to help diagnose any problems that your horse might have with direct turn. As you are riding your shallow loops you're going to ask yourself does my horse turn as easily to the left as to the right? Does he speed up or slow down either way? Does he have the same amount of bend in his neck both ways? If he speeds up or slows down you're going to correct that before and after each turn. If he's heavy to turn in one direction you're going to make the second part of your signal a little bit stronger to motivate him to turn a little more quickly. If he's really dull and his turns are delayed you might even have to vibrate your turning rein a little bit to motivate him to turn. But once he's turning well, make sure you make your turn signal light again.

Riding shallow loops in both directions - a wiggly line all the way around your working area - is a great way to diagnose any problems in your turn responses.

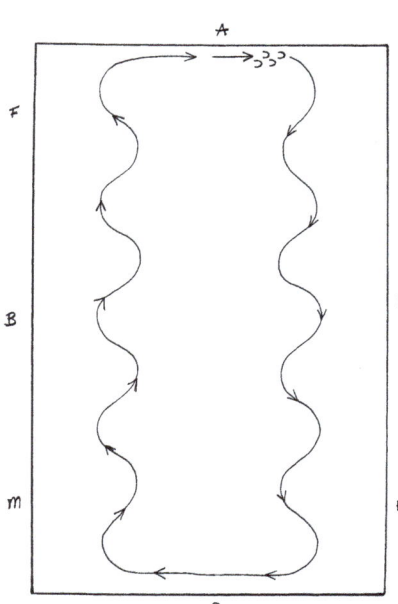

It is also important to train your horse not to turn unless he's given a signal to do so.

As well as training your horse to turn it's also really important to train your horse not to turn unless he's given the signal to do so. This is true of all the foundation responses… your horse should not stop, slow, go or turn unless given the signal to do so.

Our next training exercise is all about not turning, which means it's about staying straight. At the walk, pick a point in your working area and ride your horse on an imaginary line towards it. If he drifts away from your line, correct him by using your turn signals. We call this the line game. You will probably find that your horse drifts in one direction more than the other. If you can catch the drift within a stride, your horse will soon learn to travel in a straight line. You can do this exercise at trot next and eventually at canter too. If your horse continues to drift you'll need to get your metronome. Pay careful attention to his rhythm as he drifts away from your line. Changes of tempo and losses of line quite often go together. If you correct the change of tempo first, the loss of line will be easier to cure.

Riding a wiggly line around your working area is a great way to test your turn responses. Ask yourself if your horse turns as easily to the left and right? Does he speed up or slow down either way? Does he have the same amount of bend in his neck both ways? This way you can make your turns very even in each direction.

Builidng a miniature arena of about 20m x 8m is a great test of your horse's turn responses and his tempo.

Another exercise that you can use to train really reliable turn responses is to build yourself a miniature arena about 20m x 8m using marker cones or poles. Imagine that your little arena is the top of a really tall mountain with cliffs on either side – so don't let your horse step outside the lines! Ride around your arena. You'll need to pay careful attention in your corners in order to avoid falling off the mountain top. Try trotting around the arena too. You might have to start off in little trot (70bpm or slower) so that you don't fall off the mountain. Try some transitions from trot to walk and from walk to trot. Once you're really good at those try some school figures on your scaled down arena. Start with changing the rein across the (little tiny) diagonal and work your way up to three loop serpentines. Then add your metronome. If you can ride a three loop serpentine on the little arena without a change of rhythm, you have achieved ninja status and are ready to start indirect turn.

If you can ride a three loop serpentine on the little arena without a change of rhythm, you have achieved ninja status and you're ready to start indirect turn.

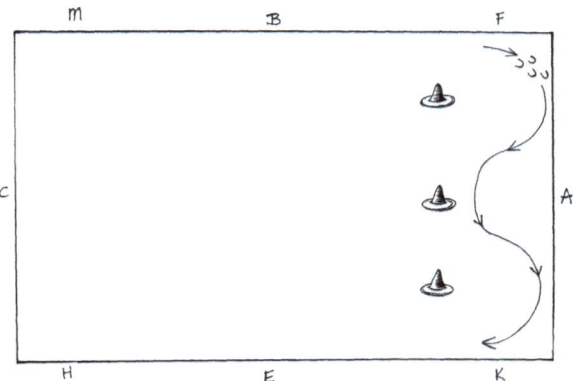

Indirect Turn

To learn about indirect turn you'll have to get down on your hands and knees again. Look to the left but make your shoulders go to the right. The first step will be an adducting one with your left arm / foreleg and the second step will be an abducting one with your right arm / foreleg. This is indirect turn. In an indirect turn the first step is an adducting one. In a direct turn the first step is an abducting one.

The first step of an indirect turn is an adducting one. That is, the horse's leg moves towards his body.

> ## Did you know?
> Once you have mastered stop, go, turn and indirect turn you'll have really good control of your horse's front legs. You can now ask them to move forwards, backwards, abduct (move away from his body) and adduct (move towards his body). If he does this from light cues he is now very obedient. This will also help him to be calm.

The cue for indirect turn is taking both of your hands in the direction you want to go. Your horse should look slightly in one direction, while turning in the other direction.

Once you have good stop, go, turn and indirect turn responses from light aids your horse will be obedient and calm.

To train indirect turn, ride around your working area, about one metre from the outside track. Take both your hands towards the outside track. In the beginning, to get your horse's shoulders to move towards the outside track you'll probably have to apply a little bit more pressure on the outside rein. However, because your inside rein is against your horse's neck he should be looking a little bit to the inside while he is moving his shoulders to the outside. You might have to practise this a few times before you get it right.

Eventually your indirect turn cue will become very subtle, just the movement of your inside hand towards his wither.

Eventually your goal is to train your horse so that just closing your inside hand against his neck (your hand is just above his wither) will cause his inside front leg to adduct. It really helps if you can apply the indirect turn cue as his inside front leg is in the swing phase.

The best time to apply the indirect turn cue is as his inside front leg is in the swing phase.

You'll find indirect turn useful in a variety of situations, including riding deeper into the corners, and correcting falling in.

When you can do indirect turn one way, change the rein and try it the other way too. You can try leaving a larger gap between your horse and the outside track to make the exercise more challenging. You can also ride your horse on a small circle of about 10 metres diameter and then, using indirect turn, spiral out to a 20 metre circle. Once you can do that on both reins add your metronome and check that your horse doesn't lose his rhythm during the turn.

Although you will use your direct turn far more often, you can use indirect turn in lots of situations. You can use it to help your horse travel a little bit more deeply into corners. You can also use it to correct "falling in" which is when a horse travels on a circle and always seems to be making that circle smaller. When training canter signals with young horses you can use indirect turn to help your horse achieve slight flexion at the poll to the inside, which will encourage him to take the correct lead at canter.

> ### Indirect turn vs. direct turn...
> You need to keep direct and indirect turn really clear and separate. Remember, the first step of a direct turn is an abducting step and the first step of an indirect turn is an adducting step.

When you're riding or leading your horse, he should always be travelling in the direction that you want him to, that is, he should always be on your imaginary line. This demonstrates well trained turn responses. Your horse should also stay in the tempo that you choose – he shouldn't always be speeding up or slowing down. This demonstrates good stop and go responses. If you can ride your horse on your line at your tempo with light signals at walk trot and canter it's pretty likely that you have great foundation responses. Well done! We can now start the fun stuff! Jumping!

If you can ride your horse on your line, at your tempo, with light signals at walk, trot and canter it's pretty likely that you have great foundation responses.

Here's a place for you to write stuff!

Chapter Eleven

Jumping and other really fun stuff

Jumping is a great way to test the stop, go forwards and turn responses that you have trained. It doesn't matter if you have a prize winning show horse, a hairy pony or even a unicorn – correct foundation responses will make jumping safer and much more fun.

Before you begin jumping, you should test your foundation responses in a few different environments, including the place where you plan to do your jumping. In chapter three we talked about your horse's memory and how unfamiliar things in familiar places (like a wheelbarrow on the arena) can make him very suspicious and ready to run away. He might be quite surprised when you walk him out to your riding area and there are new poles or jumps in it. If your horse is the type to get really frightened by new things it's a good idea to do some ground work near the jumps before you start to ride.

Before you begin jumping, you should test your foundation responses in a few different environments.

Before you begin jumping, you should test your foundation responses in a few different places, including the place where you plan to do your jumping. Be sure to test your responses on the ground and under saddle near your jumps, too!

Throughout the exercises in this chapter, it is important that you always try to maintain a constant rhythm. If your horse speeds up towards the jump it isn't because he loves jumping. He is expressing the flight response because he is frightened or unsure. Ensuring a steady and consistent rhythm will help your horse to stay calm. It will also help to keep you safe because if your horse increases in speed by a little bit after each obstacle he will be going very fast by the end of a 10 jump course!

Your horse needs to have his neck in its natural posture when jumping. This is very important for his vision.

What about self carriage?
Some people think that self carriage is just for dressage horses but it's just as important when jumping. Your horse should be able to maintain his rhythm and stay on your line before you start jumping.

Your horse needs to have his neck in its natural posture when jumping. This is very important because the horse's vision is different to ours and he'll need to be able to carry his head in a way that enables him to see the jump and assess where he needs to take off.

Some people think that self carriage is just for dressage horses but it's just as important when jumping.

A neck-strap is just an old stirrup leather fastened loosely around your horse's neck. It can be a very useful tool, especially while learning to jump!

You need all the same safety equipment for jumping, especially your helmet. Wearing a body protector is also very wise and a neck-strap can be a very useful tool and is certainly not just for beginners!

You'll need the same safety equipment for jumping as you do for your normal riding activities. Helmet and riding boots are a must and it is very wise to also wear a body-protector and use a neck-strap for added safety. A neck-strap is just an old stirrup leather fastened loosely around your horse's neck so that you can hold on to it if you become unbalanced, or while in the air over a jump. That way you won't accidentally apply rein aids that you didn't mean to when you are jumping.

Poles

Poles are like a miniature version of a jump, so once you have checked that your horse's responses are light in hand and under saddle, we're going to begin testing your foundation responses over a single pole at walk, trot and canter. It is important to always remember that the pole (or jump) only signals to the horse that he should lift his legs a little higher, it shouldn't signal the need for speeding up, slowing down or veering off your line.

Poles are like a miniature version of a jump, so they are a great place to start.

Before you begin jumping you should be able to walk, trot and canter over a single pole without any change in the rhythm.

Place your pole on the ground and walk your horse towards it on a straight line. Let him look at it if it frightens him but don't let him look or turn away from it because his lack of object permanence makes that quite reinforcing for him. In the horse's brain it might work a little bit like this... didn't like pole, turned away from pole, pole went away. By turning away from the pole your horse makes the pole go away. This will make him much more likely to turn away from a pole in the future. If you think this sounds like negative reinforcement you are completely correct! Remember that you get the behaviour you reinforce, not necessarily the behaviour you want. If you let your horse turn away from the pole you are reinforcing turning away from the pole. This is one reason why it's important to have really good foundation responses before you start jumping.

Let your horse look at the pole if it frightens him but don't let him turn away. Remember - for the horse, out of sight really is out of mind, so it's quite reinforcing for him if he gets to turn away from the pole.

Keep your usual light contact on the reins and don't lean forward over the pole.

If your horse's responses get a little heavier than normal, it just means that the pole is overshadowing his training.

If your horse's responses get a little heavier than normal, it just means that the pole is overshadowing his training. Do lots of downwards transitions both before and after the pole until he no longer changes his rhythm. Some horses will happily walk over a pole the first time they see one, while others will need dozens of repetitions over many days before they will calmly walk over it.

Don't forget...
Use lots of positive reinforcement in the form of wither scratching when you are training your horse under saddle.

If your horse is rushing, it's more likely that his downward transition will be heavy. Use the metronome to check your tempo.

Put single poles in different places all over your working area and walk over them. Use your metronome to check for changes of tempo. Once your horse can walk calmly over the poles, you can start trotting. Similarly, if he quickens, do lots of downward transitions. Pay particular attention to downward transitions immediately after the poles. If your horse is rushing, it's more than likely this transition will be heavy. Continue with downward transitions until he is light again. Use your metronome to check that your tempo is staying consistent. Once you can maintain 75bpm you can also vary the tempo and use slow trot over the poles too.

Test that you can ride downward transitions using light cues before and after the pole. Remember to try it with the pole in lots of different places on your working area.

Try very hard to never let your horse veer around a pole. This is why it's really important to have your turn responses well established before you start jumping. If your horse starts to swerve away from the pole when trotting, do a downward transition and then walk him over the pole. It's easier to correct his line at walk because everything happens much more slowly!

Never let your horse veer around a pole. This is why it is really important to have your turn responses well established before you start jumping.

Don't forget...
Your horse doesn't know that there is an option to go around the pole to the left or the right so don't let him in on the secret by letting him take that option even once. No one else is going to tell him the secret if you don't!

Once you are able to trot over poles without losing rhythm and line you can begin to canter them. Start with just a single pole on a 20 metre circle. If your horse quickens, do downward transitions – paying particular attention to the transition after the pole. Make sure that you can ride a downward transition to halt about 10 metres after the pole without swerving from your line. If you can't do this it's probably because the pole is overshadowing your horse's training. Go back to trotting over poles and work on making your horse's transitions lighter.

Use your metronome to check how consistent your horse's tempo is in walk, trot and canter over the pole.

Get your metronome out and check that your horse is maintaining his 95bpm tempo while cantering over poles. Once you can keep a steady tempo on a 20 metre circle, practise with your poles on straight lines as this is often harder.

Your horse's canter stride is much longer than his trot stride, which means he won't always arrive at the pole at the perfect distance. Don't try to adjust his stride on the way to the pole. Instead, focus on keeping a steady rhythm and staying on your line.

Your horse's canter stride is much longer than his trot stride, which means he won't always arrive at the pole at the perfect distance. Don't try to adjust his stride on the way to the pole. As a rider your job is to keep your horse in a steady rhythm and on your imaginary line. Your horse's job is to coordinate his legs

If your horse does an awkward canter stride over the pole, try not to interfere with him. Stay in an upright position and, if needed, hold on to the neck strap. He'll soon learn to find his distances more consistently.

to enable him to jump. We call this foot work. Some horses are really good at working out where their legs need to be to jump and others take time to learn, but they're all better at it than most riders. If your horse does an awkward canter stride over the pole, try not to interfere with him or pull on his mouth. Stay in an upright seat and hold onto the neck strap.

It is your horse's job to coordinate his legs to enable him to jump. We call this foot work.

If you can walk, trot and canter over single poles without your horse changing tempo or losing line and you remain balanced even when your horse has to change the length of his stride over the pole, you are ready to begin jumping.

Once you can maintain your line and tempo over poles at walk, trot and canter you are ready to begin jumping.

Types of show jumps

Cross rail – very useful for teaching the horse to stay straight and always jump in the middle of the jump.

Vertical or upright – a straightforward fence, great for warming up and early training.

There are several different types of jumps your horse will see when jumping. He needs to learn about these jumps while he is still jumping small fences, so that they don't frighten him once they are bigger.

Oxer – the width of an oxer adds to the technical difficulty as the horse needs to judge the width as he approaches the fence and put in the correct amount of effort required.

Swedish Oxer – these fences can be very hard for the horse to judge and is best jumped only when you and your horse are quite experienced.

Triple Bar - triple bar jumps are like an oxer with an extra bit. They can be quite wide, especially at the base.

Double – two fences that are either one or two strides apart, typically made up of two vertical fences or a vertical and an oxer.

Treble – three fences that are either one or two strides apart, these are very tricky and usually only jumped by the more experienced.

Related line or related distance – two fences between 3 and 7 strides apart.

Fill – usually colourful and exciting, fill is anything decorative that is placed on, under or near the jump. Sometimes fill can be in the form of a water tray, dazzle board, road cones or pot plants.

Jumping at the trot

As we know, the horse's brain is very different to ours and that affects his ability to process information in a hurry. It is important to give your horse lots of time to see the jump, check the footing and decide how to negotiate the obstacle when we first introduce him to jumping exercises. For this reason, we start jumping at the trot, rather than the canter. By beginning with trot jumping we give our horses plenty of time to look at the jump and see that the take off and landing are safe, and that there are no imaginary lions hiding under the jump. We also give ourselves plenty of time to react if the horse starts to speed up, slow down or veer left or right in reaction to the jump.

Give your horse lots of time to see the jump when first introducing your horse to jumping.

Begin by approaching the jump in trot so that you have plenty of time to react if the horse begins to veer off your line, or change his rhythm.

Starting with the same pole you were using when when you mastered the art of walking, trotting and cantering over a single pole, we're now going to work on trotting over a small jump. It doesn't matter how small the jump is to start with, your horse doesn't mind how small he jumps and you can always make it bigger once you have become an expert at it.

It doesn't matter how small the jump is to start with, your horse doesn't mind!

Nerd word alert!
Some people have very fancy jumping equipment but it is ok to improvise, as long as the objects you are using to prop your poles up are safe, free from sharp edges and have no places where your horse could get his hoof caught if he bumps into it.

Remember to look up and ahead when you jump, and be sure to have elastic elbows so your horse can move his neck to balance.

You're aiming to maintain the same tempo in the approach and getaway.

A cross-rail is a great jump to start with because it will help to teach you and your horse to stay in the middle of the jump. Begin by trotting over the cross rail at a low height and progress to slightly bigger if you feel comfortable. You might impress your friends if you jump higher, but your horse is just as happy jumping small things until you both get the hang of it. You're aiming to maintain the same tempo in the approach and getaway, this way we know that your horse is not frightened of the jump, and he doesn't think it is a signal to go faster.

Progress to different types of jumps only once you have mastered simple fences. You want training to be as uneventful as possible so take small steps towards your goal height. Stick to trotting your jumps until you reach ninja status!

It is important to teach your horse to jump all the different styles of jump he might see during his jumping career while training at the smallest level.

When you have mastered the cross rail, you can progress to small verticals, oxers and even coloured fill. Remember to start small with each different type of jump you introduce to your horse's training – no bigger than 45cm. It's important to start by teaching your horse to jump all the different styles of jump he might see during his jumping career at a small level (and from trot) and progress to higher jumps slowly.

While it is important not to get left behind and hang on to the reins (and therefore your horse's mouth) for balance over a jump, it is also important not to lean too far forward. Not only are we more likely to fall off in the event of a refusal or run-out if we are leaning forward, it also makes your horse's job of clearing the jump more difficult. Remember playing on the see-saw in the playground at school when you were younger? Now imagine the horse as a big, furry see-saw. If you sit on the front of the see-saw (lean forward) the front of the see-saw usually goes down, doesn't it? So, sit on the back of the see-saw (sitting up tall, with your shoulders back), and the front must come up – like it does when your horse lifts himself up over a jump.

Imagine your horse as a big, furry see-saw. You want to sit up tall so that you are sitting on the back of the see-saw, allowing your big, furry see-saw to jump successfully and easily!

While you don't want to get left behind and pull on the reins for balance, it is also important not to lean too far forward over the jumps as you may unbalance your horse.

When you can trot over all the different types of fences and halt between 6 and 10 metres after the jump from light aids you know you're ready to progress to cantering over jumps!

You should be able to halt within 6 to 10 metres after each fence from a light aid.

A note on giving the horse a lead over jumps

Did you know that no-one has ever been able to prove that horses can learn to do new things by watching other horses? While horses often follow each other and do things together (like drinking or grazing), they won't learn new behaviours because they have been standing in the yard next to the arena watching other horses have jumping lessons.

This means that while it can be beneficial to let your horse follow another horse over a new or scary looking jump, he is not learning to do it because he is watching the other horse jump the fence – he is simply more inclined to go in that direction because his friend is also going in that direction. This makes it a useful tool for introducing horses to new things, but we need to be sure that we can always accomplish the task on our own as well – this is the ultimate test of the foundation responses.

Allowing a horse to follow another horse can be a useful training tool but it is not a substitute for good foundation responses.

Jumping at the canter

It is really important for your horse that you take small steps in training, not giant leaps.

Once you've mastered jumping from trot and your horse stays calm and obedient over all sorts of different shapes and styles of jumps, you're ready to progress to jumping from canter.

By now, you'll have seen a pattern emerging – you will always start the next step of training using familiar things from the step before. In this instance, you're going to begin by using exactly the same jumps that you used for jumping from trot to begin the cantering exercises. This way, the only new part of the exercise is the speed of approach, as your horse is already familiar with the jumps. It is really important for your horse that you take small steps in training, not giant leaps.

Once you can confidently canter over small jumps without losing rhythm or line you can get creative with the types of jumps you tackle.

Once you can canter over small jumps without losing rhythm or line you can be as adventurous as you like with the types and shapes and colours of jumps you attempt. Just remember, it is always good to approach new jumps in trot and start with them as low as possible – low enough so that if your horse gets a fright he can still walk over the jump.

Later on, we'll talk about some ways you can correct (and prevent) any problems you may come across in your jumping training such as rushing or becoming crooked.

Exercises to try...

5, 4, 3, 2, 1 blast off!

Counting down to a single pole is a really helpful exercise to develop your 'jumping eye' so that you can more easily predict when your horse is going to take off over a jump. We don't want to tell him where to take off, or interfere with him on the approach to the jump, but if you know when he'll jump it's easier to sit in a balanced position.

With a single pole on the ground, approach in either trot or canter and see if you can say "one" on the take off stride. If you can master that a few times in a row, try saying "two, one" on the last two strides before take off. You can keep going until you're saying "five, four, three, two, one" for the last five strides before take off if you're very clever!

> *We don't want to tell the horse where to take off, or interfere with him on the approach to the jump, but if you know when he'll jump it's easier to sit in a balanced position.*

If you have reached wizard level and can count down from five at canter five times in a row with no mistakes you can make the pole into a small jump and see if you're still a wizard.

Counting strides between poles

Place two poles on the ground in a straight line around 20-25 metres apart. Start by walking or trotting over them and count how many steps your horse takes between the two poles. Once you've mastered that, try shortening your horse's step and see if you can get him to take more steps than last time. You can do the opposite too and lengthen his step to see if you can get him to take less steps. It doesn't really matter how many steps your horse takes, just that you can make him take a few more and a few less.

It is useful to be able to lengthen and shorten your horse's stride between two poles, or jumps.

You can do this in canter too. It's much harder in canter so it is a good challenge.

The circle challenge

Set yourself a rhythm and line challenge by putting 4 small jumps on a 20 or 30 metre circle. Imagine your circle is a clock face and place your poles at 12 o'clock, 3 o'clock, 6 o'clock and 9 o'clock. Start with poles and then progress to small cross-rails. Begin in trot and once you can do the exercise without losing rhythm or line you can progress to canter.

Jumping on a turn is a great way to prove how good your turn responses are.

The square challenge

Now, build a square that is about 30 metres across using cones or something similar. Place your poles in the middle of each side of your square. Focus on riding really good direct turns so that you are straight for the poles and your horse has time to see the pole. It's really useful for testing your direct turns each way and for helping to quicken your horse's reactions so that he can easily find his footing if he gets to a fence in a muddle. That's a really important skill to have once you start cross-country training.

Training your horse to jump skinnies is a really good way to test your training.

Skinnies

Narrow fences or skinnies are about 1.2 metres wide. Training your horse to jump skinnies is a really good way to test your training. Always start with the skinny jump small enough so that you can walk over it if you need to. It's very important not to let the horse learn to run-out to the side of the jump, so start at walk or slow trot.

Trouble shooting...
Rushing

It is often claimed that horses that rush their fences are just excited to be jumping. Unfortunately rushing is simply an expression of the flight response so it is very important that you train your horse not to quicken. If given no alternatives, the horse will run towards an object that frightens him, not just away from it. So rushing in the approach or getaway from a jump is an indication that the horse is nervous, frightened or unsure of the task at hand.

Rushing, while commonly mistaken for excitement, is actually an expression of the flight response.

It is important to deal with any rushing on the landing side of the jump.

A horse that rush when jumping is exhibiting the flight response just as clearly as one that is running away from a hungry lion.

It is important to deal with any rushing on the landing side of the jump, not the takeoff side. If you start pulling on the reins in the last few strides before takeoff your horse may change his head position which can make it harder for him to see the fence and which, in turn, makes jumping very dangerous.

Make sure you can halt 6-10 metres after each jump from a light aid.

> *Drifting indicates that there is a problem with direct turn and is best tackled by heading back to basics.*

Go back to trotting over jumps until you have more control of the speed and line. Make sure you are able to halt within 6 to 10 metres after the jump each time. Once you can very easily do this at trot, try it at canter. Remember, the most important part of the aid is the release – so be sure to release the instant he stops and reward him by scratching his neck once he's halted.

Drifting left or right over the jump

When your horse drifts to the left or right in the approach or while jumping it can be very hard to find your way to the next fence! It can also become a bigger problem later (see running out below), so it is best re-trained early on.

Drifting indicates that there is a problem with direct turn and is best tackled by heading back to basics. Go back through all the turn exercises from chapter ten and make sure your horse will turn from light signals. Pay particular attention to the not turning exercise at both trot and canter. There's a pretty good chance that you'll find your horse drifts a little bit from your line even when there's no jump. Once you're really good at not turning you'll find it much easier to eliminate the drift. If you have noticed the drift early enough you'll find it easy to fix, because it won't have become a habit.

Most horses that run out will veer to the same side almost every time.

Cross-rails will help to prevent and correct a horse that drifts, but it is also important to go back and improve your turn responses.

Jump plenty of cross-rails, as these will help to keep you and your horse aimed at the middle of the jump (because this is the lowest part). If you're very established in your jumping position and you feel balanced, you can gently apply the opposite turning aid over the jump (for example, if your horse has been drifting to the left, you could quietly open the right rein in the approach to help stop your horse from drifting (turning) to the left. Making a runway (about 1.2 metres wide) out of marker cones on both sides of the jump can also help to correct drift.

Running out

When a horse runs out (veers to the left or right of the jump, instead of jumping it), it indicates a fault in the horse's direct turn responses. Most horses will run out in the same direction each time. If your horse runs out to the left, there is a problem with the right direct turn signal, and the same in reverse – if your horse runs out to the right, you need to work on your horse's left direct turn response. It's really just a bigger version of the drifting we spoke about before. It's just that in this instance the horse drifts so far before the fence that he avoids jumping it. Running out almost always goes together with quickening, usually in the approach to the fence. It is important to fix the quickening first and then, using the exercises for the drifting horse, fix the running out.

> *Stopping is a warning sign that your horse's training is not as thorough as the jump is high.*

Stopping or refusing

During chapter three we talked about object permanence. When you're jumping it's important to understand object permanence because if your horse refuses a jump and you turn him away in order to approach the fence again, you have effectively removed the fence and reinforced his stopping behaviour. For this reason, it is much more beneficial to keep him in front of the fence, and step backwards a few paces until you can trot forward over the jump. If you need to, have your friend or helper lower the fence so you can safely jump it from trot or walk, from a few paces away. Stopping is a warning sign that your horse's training is not as thorough as the jump is high. If your horse starts stopping at fences it is time to go back and train over lower fences until he is obedient and calm again.

> *Punishment doesn't tell the horse what to do. It only tells him what not to do.*

> *Twenty seconds of anger when you're training your horse can take weeks and even months to undo.*

A note about punishment...

Sometimes you'll see people giving their horse a smack with the whip when he runs out or refuses at a jump. This is positive punishment. Punishment can be quite a big problem and in this case is best avoided because it doesn't give the horse any clues about what to do instead of the incorrect behaviour. For example, if you smack the horse with the whip for stopping he might try something that you like even less, like bucking, or running away from the jump. He is also very likely to form an association between the punishment and the thing that caused it (in this case, the jump) and he may then become more frightened of it and even less likely to jump it. Or may start rushing towards or after the jump in order to avoid it.

Most riders love their horses and they wouldn't use punishment if they really understood what a problem it can be and how much of a surprise party it is. People generally only use punishment when they don't know what else to do or if they're angry. It's very important not to get angry when you're training your horse because it can lead to bad decisions and lots of surprise parties. Twenty seconds of anger when you're training your horse can take weeks and even months to undo.

Chapter Twelve

More fun stuff: Cross Country

Cross country riding is a very good test of the foundation responses you have trained. Cross country riding requires your horse to jump obstacles of all shapes and sizes, including into water, over ditches, and up and down banks. While he is naturally capable of doing all these things, if he was galloping through the bush on his own he might be inclined to go around the obstacles and would probably avoid leaping into the water!

If your horse was galloping in the bush on his own he might be inclined to avoid leaping into the water!

Did you know?
Eventing was originally devised to test the horses of military officers to determine their fitness and suitability for battle. The dressage was a test of elegance and obedience in preparation for parading while the cross country tested stamina, bravery and courage over difficult terrain and obstacles – important for long marches or if a horse was asked to carry a dispatch across country or through battle. The role of the final phase of showjumping, usually held on the next day, was to prove the horse's soundness and fitness following the difficult cross-country efforts.

The first appearance of eventing as an Olympic sport was in 1912 and it was originally only open to male military officers in active duty, mounted only on military charges. Eventing has seen many changes over the decades to accommodate modern ideas of sport and is now a much-shortened format comprising a dressage test, shortened cross country test and a showjumping round. It is usually held over one or two days and can range from 30cm classes to an international level called Four Star where the jumps can be as big as 1.20m high (or 1.45m with brush) and 2.0m wide.

Training a horse to jump big cross country fences takes many years and lots and lots of work.

Types of Cross Country Jumps

Logs – these can be all shapes and sizes but they are one of the easiest cross country fences as they are natural looking and usually an inviting shape.

Spreads – these are usually like the oxers we spoke about in the jumping chapter, only made from wood or logs, but they can also be table-tops, roll-tops, or house shaped jumps.

Eventing at the highest level can be very technical and the jumps can be as big as 1.20m high and 2.0m wide.

Brush – any fence that has a soft hedge through which the horses can 'brush' their legs. Sometimes it looks like the witch's parking lot because it could be a row of witch brooms all lined up!

Ditches are said to be 'rider frighteners' because they usually scare the riders more than the horses.

Ditches – a long, narrow hole in the ground, like a trench. Sometimes you have to jump an open ditch, and sometimes it will have a jump built above it. They are said to be 'rider frighteners' because they usually scare the riders more than the horses.

Coffin – this is a combination of usually three jumps, with a ditch in the middle. They are often built on steep terrain making it hard for the horse to negotiate. They are for experienced combinations.

Water jump – the part of the cross country course where we get to go splash! Water jumps are not very deep (usually only 20-30cm), but your horse doesn't know that so he might be frightened about entering the water initially.

At the higher levels you'll be required to jump down a bank into water. Sometimes this will also have brush on it.

Banks or steps – you may have to jump either up or down banks or steps and your approach and technique will differ significantly depending on the direction. Banks are often seen in a water jump, where at the higher levels you will jump down the drop in to the water.

Skinny – these are narrow jumps designed to test the obedience and accuracy of horse and rider. They're easy to run out at, and usually placed in difficult locations on the course such as after a drop or water jump or around a tight corner. They are mostly seen at the higher levels but that doesn't mean you can't train over some miniature skinnies in preparation!

Skinnies, apexes and combinations that require you to jump on an angle are the ultimate test of your line.

Apex – these are triangle shaped jumps and can be very tricky. They're designed to test the accuracy of the rider and obedience of the horse as there is usually only a small jumpable part near the edge, inviting a run-out if your horse is not very good at staying on your line.

Owl holes or key holes – these can be particularly frightening for the horse because he has to jump through them. They are usually made with brush.

Cross-country training can be very time consuming because your horse will need lots of repetitions of each kind of obstacle.

Cross Country Basics

If you want to take your horse cross country it's very important to start slowly. Your horse needs to learn how to negotiate lots of different types of obstacles and the best way for him to do this is from the walk and trot. If you've worked through the jumping exercises in this book you already know how to introduce your horse to cross country fences because you've already introduced him to showjumping fences.

Walking up and down small banks, over ditches and through the water is the best way to start cross country training.

Cross country training can be very time consuming because your horse will need lots of repetitions of each kind of obstacle before he learns how to jump each one reliably. He will need to practise on at least four or five different ditches, four or five different banks and four or five different water jumps. You can also use natural terrain to help train him – even making him walk through puddles instead of going around them will help him learn important cross country skills.

Spend plenty of time walking up and down small banks, over small ditches and through the water. See if you can halt your horse with his feet in the ditch if it is shallow enough.

Even the quietest horse can find a ditch terrifying when asked to walk over it.

Begin by walking up and down small banks, over small ditches and through water. Your aim is to sit very still and give the horse time to stretch his neck down and look at the obstacle as he approaches it. He should stay in an even rhythm and, as always, stay on your line, so while you're sitting quietly letting him assess the question on approach, you're also ready to correct any reactions he gives you such as a small swerve or a change in speed. If you're going slowly enough you'll have plenty of time to react to changes as they happen.

Even the quietest horses can find a ditch terrifying when asked to walk over it. Be patient and start with a small and shallow ditch. The time you spend training your horse calmly now will be more than rewarded in the years to come.

It is important to stay tall in the saddle and not lean forward.

Once you can safely negotiate small, single cross country obstacles at the walk you can trot. In a wide open space like a cross country course, trotting might make your horse excited and you should be prepared to do lots of downward transitions – particularly after each obstacle. The same rules apply to both jumping and cross country training so use the troubleshooting sections from chapter eleven to help address any problems that come up.

Allow your horse to adjust his own stride on the way to the fence.

When approaching cross country obstacles it's important to stay tall in the saddle and not lean forward. Allow your horse to adjust his own stride on the way to the fence and practise maintaining

> *Training your horse to be calm on the cross country course is of utmost importance.*

the same rhythm both before and after the fence. When you can happily trot over single cross country obstacles you can make up a short course. If your horse remains calm, keeps a steady rhythm and stays on your line over several different cross country obstacles, you're ready to try cantering.

Training your horse to be calm on the cross country course is of utmost importance. Anxiety and tension can be the result of surprise parties and are a signal that your training has some gaps in it. Check all of your horse's foundation responses using the exercises in this book and then start your cross country training back at the beginning by walking over very small obstacles until he can do that calmly. Do not increase the size of the jumps or your speed until your horse is calm and you can control him with light signals. This might take hours, days or even months of practice but it is very important, not only for his welfare but also for your safety. When your horse is anxious he is exhibiting the flight response. This changes the way that he jumps – not only will he jump more quickly but he will also be more inclined to hollow his back and not lift his front legs up over the fence. This can be extremely dangerous as cross country fences are usually fixed and do not fall down if they are hit.

> *When your horse is anxious he is exhibiting the flight response which changes the way he jumps - this can be dangerous and is usually always the result of surprise parties.*

When you start competing at events it can be very tempting to gallop around the cross country course. However, it's much more important to train your horse to trot calmly over the obstacles. It is far better for your horse's future to establish calmness first and only increase your speed when every other aspect of his cross country training is well established. The same applies to the start box – which is where you will start your cross country course. Lots of horses learn to get very anxious in the start box because their riders gallop them out of it. It is far better to walk out of the start box and then ride an upward transition to trot and then to canter – paying careful attention to rhythm and line. In this way your horse will start his cross country round the way you want him to finish it – calmly and being controlled by light signals.

> **It is tempting to gallop out of the start box and zoom around the cross country course but it is far more useful to take your time and have a calm horse. You can make up time by riding accurate and economical lines instead.**

Walking the course carefully will help you to decide on economical lines that allow you to approach the jumps well, while saving you precious seconds so you don't have to gallop fast!

Here's a place for you to write stuff!

Chapter Thirteen

Show-nopoly

Going out to competitions, clinics and training days can be great fun and a really valuable training experience for you and your horse. However, in order to avoid surprise parties, it's very important to prepare thoroughly for each outing.

It's important to avoid surprise parties when you take your horse out to competitions, clinics and training days.

Before you enter for a competition it's important that your horse's training is really reliable. When your horse goes to an unfamiliar place he may get very excited and this will cause his brain to produce a hormone called adrenaline. Adrenaline works on behaviours a little bit like fertilizer on a paddock full of weeds – it makes them grow! So… if your horse swerves a little from

Adrenaline works on behaviours a little bit like fertilizer on a paddock full of weeds.

your line at home, at a competition he might leap sideways. If your horse rushes his fences at home, at a competition he might bolt. Which means that the most important preparation for an event is to make sure that your training at home is really reliable.

Competitions are a very good test of your horse's foundation responses because there are lots of distractions for him to cope with like noise and other horses. Introducing these while you are training at home can be a great way of helping make outings less scary. You can do things like playing the radio while you ride and inviting your friends over to ride with you. It's also important that you train your horse regularly before competitions. You should be riding him three times per week at least or he is not going to be fit enough to cope with the extra work load of a competition. He should also load calmly onto a trailer and be able to cope with short journeys.

Competitions are a very good test of your horse's foundation responses.

The rest of this chapter is a series of steps that can guide you through taking your horse out to competitions. It's a little bit like the board game Monopoly because you move forwards step by step. Think of each step as a firewall – you can't go on unless you've achieved it. So you must achieve step one before moving onto step two and you must achieve step two before moving onto step three. You can't skip steps, but you can go backwards if necessary.

Show-nopoly is a bit like the board game monopoly, designed to help you take your horse to a show.

165

These steps will help you avoid surprise parties in new situations.

The steps in this chapter will help you to avoid surprise parties in new situations. They also offer some suggestions for how to manage your horse at competitions and provide a warm up routine for you to follow.

1 In the weeks leading up to the competition train your horse so that he works calmly and obediently at home through all of the exercises in chapters 6 – 10 and if you add distractions like a radio and other horses he stays calm.

Add distractions at home like a radio and other horses.

2 On the day of the competition allow yourself plenty of time. Unload your horse and find a quiet, safe place to practise your in hand foundation responses. Focus on stop and go responses initially. They may be heavy at first but if you stay calm and continue they will gradually become lighter. Use park to help achieve calmness.

Always allow yourself plenty of time on competition day so that you can quietly work through all of the steps.

3 Take your horse into the warm-up area in hand. Practise stop and go responses. Practise park in four or five different places. Practise transitions from slow walk to walk and back again. Make sure your horse is staying on your line and at your rhythm.

Ensure that your horse will park to be mounted. If he is fidgety, go back to ground work until he is calm again.

4 Back at the trailer, make sure your horse will park to be saddled then practise in hand responses with the saddle on in the warm up area. Find a quiet, safe area and ensure your horse will park to be mounted.

5 Practise stop and go responses under saddle at walk in a quiet, safe place. Your horse's responses may be heavy initially, but be patient and work through the stop and go exercises that you have been training at home and he will gradually get lighter. Practise transitions from walk to slow walk and back to walk again. Introduce direct turn in the form of shallow loops and circles. Ensure your horse's rhythm doesn't change during the turns. Practise indirect turns at walk. Continue until stop, go, direct turn and indirect turn responses are light.

Practise all of your transitions until they feel like they do when you're riding at home.

6 Practise transitions from walk to trot to walk. Practise slow trot. Introduce direct turn (shallow loops and circles) and indirect turn in trot. Practise the no turn exercise in trot. Practise park.

7 Take your horse to the warm up area and repeat steps 5 and 6.

8 Practise trot to canter transitions. Ensure your horse is maintaining rhythm and line at canter. Practise your shallow turns and large circles at canter. Introduce indirect turn at canter.

9 If you are competing in dressage or showing classes, your horse is now ready for you to practise any responses that are specific to your discipline – such as leg yield. If he can do that calmly, you are ready to compete. If your competition involves jumping you should be able to work through steps 1 to 9 in at least three different venues before entering a competition and then continue.

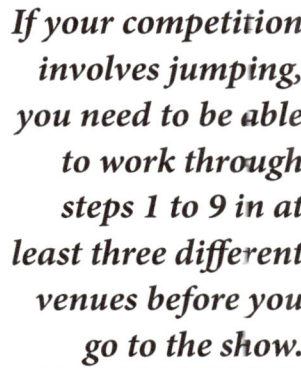

If your competition involves jumping, you need to be able to work through steps 1 to 9 in at least three different venues before you go to the show.

Always start with small jumps in the warm up. If you can, take a friend with you who can adjust the jumps for you.

10 You can work through the exercises in chapters 11 (for showjumping competitions) and chapter 12 (for eventing) calmly. You can add distractions and your horse stays calm.

11 At the competition work through steps 2 – 8. Ride your horse near to the practice fences, ensuring that he doesn't change rhythm or line.

If your horse can canter and jump calmly in the warm up arena - you're ready to compete!

12 Ask a friend to make a small cross rail for you to practise over in trot. Check that on the approach your horse stays straight and maintains his rhythm. Use downward transitions after the fence to ensure your horse is not rushing.

13 Canter the cross rail. Check that on the approach your horse stays straight and maintains his rhythm. Use downward transitions after the fence to ensure your horse is not rushing.

14 You can now practise over the other jumps in the warm up area. Ensure the jumps are small enough to approach in trot first. If your horse maintains his rhythm and line during trot, you can begin to canter. Use downward transitions if your horse begins to rush or becomes excited.

15 If your horse can canter calmly in the warm up area without loss of line or rhythm, can jump fences without quickening, refusing, running out or large losses of line – you are ready to compete!

While it's nice to win ribbons, your main goal should always be to have a calm and happy horse. He should return from the show having had a positive training experience, and definitely no surprise parties!

ACKNOWLEDGEMENTS

This book has been a collaboration between many people who gave their time, skills and expertise with great generosity. Without their help this book would not have been possible.

Many, many thanks to Barbara Hinchliffe for the amazing drawings. We are so lucky to have had the opportunity to work with an artist of her calibre. Her skill, unique world view and sense of humour were an integral part of this project.

Much gratitude must also go to our eagle-eyed proof readers Sonya Crute and Sue Warren. We are also very grateful to Nicki Stuart and Manuela McLean who gave great advice on the finished manuscript and to Jodie Vance who helped with the early drafts.

We owe many thanks to photographer extraordinaire Mandy Smith who took the lovely training photos and to Alyson and Mark Ayre who let us use their beautiful property. We must also thank our models Catherine Ayre and Piper, Charlotte Ayre and Jasper, Clancy Mercer and Timmy and, Isla Smith and Shifty.
You guys are awesome – thank you!

Credit and thanks to Red McQueen for allowing us to use a wide range of his excellent competition photographs (www.redfoto.com.au). Thank you also to Kelly and William Newton-Wordsworth for letting us use the photos of the Williams River horses, to Jody Hartstone for the great photos of Ali Baba, to Melissa Bücheler Photography for her lovely photos and to Caroline McLeod for the gorgeous photo of Lord Deniro for the Show-nopoly chapter.

We would both like to give a very special thank you to Dr Andrew McLean, not only for the foreword, but also for his knowledge, generosity and wisdom. Andrew works tirelessly to improve welfare by promoting the findings of Equitation Science and he is a staunch and fearless advocate for the horse. Andrew is also on the board of the charity HELP and he has done a great deal to improve the welfare of elephants around the world.

Lastly, and most importantly, we would like to thank all of our clients and students – who teach us at least as much as they are taught and who encourage us to be our best every day.

The person who drew the pictures...

Barbara Hinchliffe is an artist who has many years of riding experience. Barb's love for horses and sense of fun are evident in her equestrian art. She is available for commissions and portraits — you can track her down as Barbara Hinchliffe Artist on Facebook.

Sustainable Equitation

Sustainable Equitation is about small footprint horse training. It's a place where we share ideas and discoveries about ethical training, the rider as an athlete and the wider community. It's about training the less than perfect horse, travelling, connecting with others and staying healthy. Visit **www.sustainableequitation.com.au** to find out more!

Human Elephant Learning Programs (HELP)

Did you know that there are many thousands of working elephants in Asia? Some of them work in the timber industry or in national parks looking for poachers. HELP is a not-for-profit organisation that aims to improve the welfare of these elephants by implementing evidence-based training strategies very similar to the ones that you have seen in this book. HELP provides training advice and supplies training manuals for elephant trainers in India, Thailand, Myanmar and Nepal. Just as in horse training, when the welfare of the elephants improves, so too does the safety of the handlers. This makes HELP's work very important. Part of the proceeds of this book will be donated to HELP to assist with the ongoing work that they do. If you would like to learn more please go to **www.h-elp.org**.

The people who wrote this book...

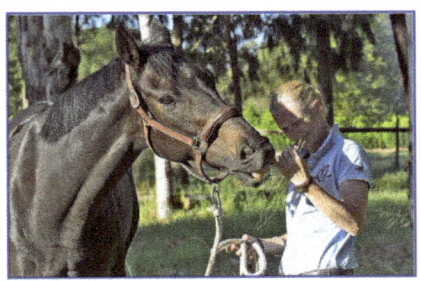

Sophie Warren is a professional event rider, horse trainer and coach. She has had many successes at the highest level in eventing and has been in the top ten placings at all of Australia's major competitions. She also represented Australia as a young rider, was Western Australian young rider of the year and her horse, Let's Impress, was Western Australian horse of the year. Sophie has ridden at FEI level in dressage and two of her mounts have won Western Australian dressage horse of the year. Sophie has ridden professionally and trained in Europe.

Dr Portland Jones is a writer, horse trainer and NCAS level 1 coach. She has competed to advanced level in dressage and lectured extensively on equine behaviour to all ages from pony club to university. Portland has written widely for both equestrian and mainstream publications. She has worked with equine behaviourist Dr Andrew McLean for over 15 years, has a Diploma of Equitation Science and is passionate about promoting the welfare of the horse through the use of evidence-based training strategies. She is a novelist and is also on the board of the charity Human Elephant Learning Programs (HELP).

Portland and Sophie run a horse training and coaching business in Western Australia's Swan Valley. They offer foundation training for young horses as well as remedial and ongoing training. They run clinics, lectures and training days for all levels of rider. They also write articles and blogs for their website www.sustainableequitation.com.au.

www.ingramcontent.com/pod-product-compliance
Lightning Source LLC
Chambersburg PA
CBHW061137010526
44107CB00069B/2970